W9-ABF-839

CRIMINAL JUSTICE ETHICS

Also Available in
Research and Bibliographical Guides in Criminal Justice

Criminal Activity in the Deep South, 1700-1930: An Annotated Bibliography
A. J. Wright, compiler

CRIMINAL JUSTICE ETHICS

Annotated Bibliography
and
Guide to Sources

COMPILED BY
FRANK SCHMALLEGER

With the Assistance of Robert McKenrick

Research and Bibliographical Guides
in Criminal Justice, Number 2
Marilyn Lutzker, Series Adviser

GREENWOOD PRESS
New York • Westport, Connecticut • London

APR 0 9 2002

Library of Congress Cataloging-in-Publication Data

Schmalleger, Frank.
    Criminal justice ethics : annotated bibliography and guide to sources /
compiled by Frank Schmalleger with the assistance of Robert
McKenrick.
        p.   cm.—(Research and bibliographical guides in criminal
justice, ISSN 1042-4636 ; no. 2)
    Includes indexes.
    ISBN 0-313-26791-X (alk. paper)
    1. Criminal justice, Administration of—United States—Moral and
ethical aspects—Bibliography. I. McKenrick, Robert. II. Title.
III. Series.
Z5703.4.C73S36   1991
[HV9950]
174'.9364973—dc20   90-29186

British Library Cataloguing in Publication Data is available.

Library of Congress Catalog Card Number: 90-29186
ISBN: 0-313-26791-X
ISSN: 1042-4636

First published in 1991

Greenwood Press, 88 Post Road West, Westport, CT 06881
An imprint of Greenwood Publishing Group, Inc.

Printed in the United States of America

The paper used in this book complies with the
Permanent Paper Standard issued by the National
Information Standards Organization (Z39.48-1984).

10 9 8 7 6 5 4 3 2 1

This book is dedicated to Martin Gursky. Everyone calls him a living saint, but that's not saying enough; and to Brian R. Nagy, Robert McKenrick's father, who, as a stranger, took his new son into his home and heart without any reservations.

Contents

Preface

Ethical issues are of primary concern today in the field of criminal justice. Anyone who has been to recent meetings of professional groups such as the American Society of Criminology and the Academy of Criminal Justice Sciences finds that "ethics" is a key buzzword. The introductory chapter that follows defines criminal justice ethics as the term has been used in gathering material for this research and bibliographical guide and provides historical background for viewing the development of ethical awareness in criminal justice.

The pace at which any literature develops -- and this is especially true now of a literature in which there is intense interest -- verges on the phenomenal. This research guide and bibliography which seeks to capture the essence of criminal justice ethics today, would not have been possible a few short years ago. This book has bene-fited considerably from modern technological advances ranging from telecommunications to computerization. Many items were identified first through online searches of databases of the National Institute of Justice, its National Criminal Justice Reference Service, and Search Group Bulletin Board System. Both are invaluable tools for research into almost any aspect of the criminal justice system. This book has made use also of other electronic databases, including CompuServe's Information Quest and Dialog.

Once sources were identified they were often requisitioned through local libraries or inter-library loan in order to meet the traditional responsibility of the bibliographer for a "hands-on" experience with the documents to be listed. Even here new tech-nology provided frequent savings of time and effort. Inter-library loans were arranged almost instantly in most cases through computerized systems, and a fair number of documents were available for instant downloading via a modem. Hence, although this bibliography does not contain listings of "paperless books," much of what is listed here was viewed in paperless form.

Computerization does more than allow for the identification of potentially useful sources. Modern hypertextual capabilities provided either online, or by powerful desktop computers, allow the researcher to link items within databases in order to ferret out linkages which might not otherwise be apparent. However, the bulk of any research activity still depends upon the printed word, and the culmination of any useful research effort is a book like this one. Materials and ideas, once identified and linked, must still be put on paper. In this bibliography we were able to take advantage of spectacular capabilities afforded by high-quality laser printing, thus streamlining this publication process further.

As a result this bibliography is far more current and accurate than it might otherwise be; and will, we believe, be of considerable value to students, teachers, researchers, and professionals in criminal justice.

The Scope of This Guide

This bibliography has been assembled to serve those interested in teaching and/or research in the area of criminal justice ethics. It lists published books, chapters in books, articles, commission reports, videotapes, and the codes of professional and governmental organizations which substantively deal with ethical concerns in the criminal justice field. Unpublished books under contract with publishers are listed as well where it has been determined that they are nearing completion. Practicality dictated that only English language materials published in North America after 1980 could be included. However, a number of "classic" or especially significant works, known to have influenced later writings, have been incorporated even though they were produced by foreign publishers or published before 1980. Perhaps five percent of the works cited predate 1980. We did not include textbooks or lists of "standards" for criminal justice agencies (with one exception), and selected only a small number of all the materials available on the death penalty and on the moral basis of laws. Similarly excluded are works on the philosophy of law, and the proper moral reach or foundation of the law.

Because this book is intended primarily for those interested in the American *system* of criminal justice, entries are often more ideational than practical. This volume is oriented toward covering

issues. It does more than outline standards of professional behavior. It offers more citations to thought-provoking works than to
writings which concern themselves solely with the *application* of
ethical theory.   This decision was required because the sheer
quantity of material on the practical application of ethical concepts
was overwhelming and impossible to catalog in a work of this size.

On the other hand, some items have been chosen for inclusion in
this work because they deal solely with fundamental issues of
concern to thinkers on morality and justice. Writings which grap-
ple with the question of what justice means, within the context of
criminal justice administration, for example, are identified here, --
even though they may not address questions of professional behavior directly.

As an aid to research, sources of data, including electronic data
retrieval services, manuscript collections, and government repositories are identified in a separate chapter.

The Organization of This Guide: How to Use It

For purposes of this volume, we follow the traditional conventions
of: (1) viewing criminal justice as an administrative undertaking,
and (2) describing the criminal justice system in terms of its
component parts: police, courts, and corrections. Hence, the items
in this guide are presented within the framework provided by these
three categories, with "victims" added as a fourth genre. Growing
concern with the rights of communities in the face of criminal
victimization, the movement toward a victim's bill of rights which is
currently underway, and a general recognition that some balance is
needed between the constitutional guarantees accorded defendants
with the needs and interests of victims, led to a natural grouping of
bibliographic items under the heading of "victims and ethics."
Materials which deal with capital punishment, sentencing, and
probation and parole are placed in the chapter titled "corrections,"
although some are cross-referenced with the "courts" chapter.

Two indexes can be found at the end of this annotated bibliography.   One, an *author index*, lists author's names and cites entry
numbers corresponding to the desired information. Entry numbers
range from 1 to 231 beginning with the first entry and growing in
number throughout the volume. The second index, a *subject index*,
lists key words and terms of possible interest to the reader. It, too,
is primarily organized according to entry numbers. Items in either
index which refer to page numbers in the preface, the introduction,
or the last chapter (on information sources for research in criminal
justice ethics) are italicized to distinguish them from references to
entry numbers.

When looking for specific information, the user of this volume would do well to remember that criminal justice ethics is multi-dimensional. "Official" views of ethics, particularly in professional codes and compendiums dealing with behavioral standards, tend to offer a more limited perspective than is offered here.

Acknowledgments

This work would not have been possible without the able assistance of Robert McKenrick. He is a scholar and friend with, I am sure, a fascinating and rewarding career ahead of him as a lawyer. Thanks also to Kristina Rose whose work with the National Criminal Justice Reference Service has helped to move modern criminal justice research out of the dark ages and into the light of high-tech. My editor, Mildred Vasan, true professional that she is, kept this project progressing and insured a meaningful product. My wife, Celene, and daughters, Cherie and Nicole, were, as ever, understanding of the time this volume required. Their understanding has always been appreciated. Thanks also to my secretary, Wanda Hammonds, who fielded many calls and kept me in touch with the realities of both writing and teaching as this project progressed.

Introduction: The Growth of Ethical Awareness in Criminal Justice

Calls for ethical awareness in criminal justice, while by no means new, have reached a near crescendo in recent years. The professional practices of early twentieth-century police officers, correctional personnel, and judges focused typically on the apprehension of offenders and the swift and sure imposition of justice. Enforcement agents, correctional officers, and even the courts, often assumed that suspects were guilty. In an age when frontier justice was more than a recent memory, the proper punishment to be imposed claimed most of the ruminations of social philosophers. Rarely considered was the degree of "fairness" inherent in early practices.

In the 1920's when the justice system labored under the burdens imposed by Prohibition,[1] ethical concerns were given more than lip service. Prohibition created an enforcement problem which went far beyond investigation and prosecution. The vast financial holdings amassed by racketeers who were involved actively in the large-scale manufacture, transportation, and sale of illicit liquor, brought the specter of wholesale corruption to the agencies of enforcement. The Wickersham Commission, appointed in 1931 by President Herbert Hoover to explore the problems of police agencies, found that continuance of Prohibition held the potential to substantially undermine enforcement activities across the nation.[2] Police unions and fraternal organizations responded by formulating rudimentary ethical codes, calling their memberships to task, and espousing standards for the professionalization of law enforcement. The end of Prohibition and World War II drew attention away from ethical considerations in criminal justice for three decades.

Some writers trace the beginning of contemporary ethical concerns about criminal justice to the turbulent decade of the 1960's when social institutions were examined closely, and traditional practices were questioned.[3] During that period, the United States Supreme Court, led by Chief Justice Earl Warren, highlighted the rights of the accused and sought to balance them against the power of the system. The Court called to task many taken-for-granted practices in the administration of justice and focused attention on the means of *achieving* justice, rather than on the lone fact of guilt or innocence.

The courts were not alone in pressuring the criminal justice system to change. In 1967 the President's Commission on Law Enforcement and Administration of Justice, appointed by President Lyndon Johnson, submitted its final report, **The Challenge of Crime in a Free Society.** It contained a vast array of suggested improvements to be made within agencies of justice at all levels and sparked Congress to pass the Omnibus Crime Control and Safe Streets Act in 1968, which gave birth to the still-celebrated Law Enforcement Assistance Administration (LEAA). LEAA moved quickly to enhance the quality of law enforcement throughout the nation, routinely expending huge sums of money to achieve its mandate.

In 1971 Jerris Leonard, Chief Administrator of LEAA, appointed a National Advisory Commission on Criminal Justice Standards and Goals. The Commission was charged with formulating criteria for crime reduction and prevention throughout the nation. It's six volume report, delivered in 1973, set pragmatic criteria for advancing all components of the criminal justice system. Among the Commission's recommendations was a call for ethical training for police and other criminal justice specialists.[4]

Coinciding with the release of that official report was the 1973 testimony of Frank Serpico before the Knapp Commission on police corruption in New York City.[5] Serpico, an undercover operative within the police department, revealed a complex web of "protection rackets" created and maintained by unethical officers. The Knapp Commission Report distinguished between two types of corrupt officers: grass eaters and meat eaters. "Grass eating," involving mostly minor services or small bribes, was said to be relatively commonplace. "Meat eating," the other form of corruption identified by the Knapp Commission, constituted a much more serious form of corruption. It was said to involve the active seeking of illicit money-making opportunities by police officers.

While historical forms of corruption no doubt persist today, and perhaps even permeate the criminal justice system, our contemporary and rapidly evolving society has new concerns. Social change in America is occurring at a seemingly accelerated pace. The "Melting Pot" of the 1920's and 1930's has yielded to a contemporary society characterized increasingly by racial tension, economic disparity, and diverse social interests. A number of modern issues speak directly to a need for ethical awareness in criminal justice. They include: the vast array of illicit drugs inundating the country, a rapid spurt in the growth of information technology, the advent of AIDS, and the rise of extremist "hate groups."

The drug trade of the 1990's is to modern law enforcement what prohibition was to the police agencies of the 1920's. The potential for corruption wielded by drug cartels is immense since it is funded by huge financial reserves. On the other hand, the pressure to gather solid evidence and to "make a good case," combined with excessive investigative caseloads, can make even the well-meaning officer go astray. The ease with which electronic eavesdropping today permits direct access to what had heretofore been regarded as sacrosanct areas of personal privacy is unparalleled in history. Properly outfitted "listening" devices are able to record personal computer keystrokes, cordless and mobile telephone conversations, and even human voices in closed rooms, from a considerable distance with no need for old style "bugs" or hardwired connections. As a consequence, constitutional guarantees explicit in the Fourth, Fifth, and Eighth Amendments -- of the right to be secure from the unbridled investigatory activities of the government -- are in danger of being sidestepped by overzealous officials bent on bringing criminal cases to an early close. Add to this the evolution of new criminal types, including racially motivated offenders and technologically sophisticated white collar criminals, and the need for an ethically informed direction among enforcement agents becomes clear.

What Are Criminal Justice Ethics?

Before launching into the substance of this bibliography, it is useful to consider what the notion of "ethics" means in our contemporary social context. "Ethics" are, essentially, standards of behavior: specifically, standards which relate the actor, in interpersonal roles, to a set of moral criteria. They are, in other words, benchmarks for judging behavior, either one's own, or that of others, according to some measure of "goodness." Practical questions -- asking, for example, what kind of handgun is potentially most effective; what perimeter security devices will insure the fewest escapes from detention; or which software system will best serve the administrative needs of a judicial district -- are not ethical in nature. However, matters such as crowd control, the treatment of arrestees, prison conditions, the limits of investigative activity, interrogation techniques, and the presentation of evidence at trials, all have ethical aspects to them. Outright corruption aside, a number of issues are of special concern to students of criminal justice ethics today.[6] They include:

- The interests of society in protection and predictability, versus the rights of individuals to freedom of action and the pursuit of self-interest.

- The ongoing debate over capital punishment.

- Enforced drug-testing of criminal justice practitioners.

- The quandary of rendering or withholding medical assistance to/from AIDS-infected victims and/or injured offenders because of personal concerns about infection.

- The proper system response to juvenile offenders.

- Allegations of racial bias in the justice system.

- The defense duty of representing a guilty client.

- The demand for retribution as opposed to rehabilitation.

- The legal and moral perspective on so-called "victimless crimes."

- The role of women in the justice system.

In short, ethical questions deal with issues of fairness and humanity. They generally ask *why* something is being done, as well as *how* it is being accomplished. In other words, criminal justice ethics concerns itself with the *quality* of the criminal justice process, not the *quantity* of the end result.[7] Complicating the situation is the fact that answers to these questions are judged relative to standards which are often intuitive, rather than reasoned. Reasoned standards, such as the official Law Enforcement Code of Ethics,[8] are typically developed by concerned groups during an often long and arduous process of debate and are firmly set in codified form at the end of the process. More intuitive standards, however, arise far less formally and can be found in the kind of subculture which permeates professional courtroom relations and everyday correctional activities. Among informal ethical systems, the law enforcement subculture has been the most widely studied.

In addition to formal and informal sources of ethical thought, there exist various fundamental, intuitive, and theological perspectives which influence our conception of morality and which any work on ethics needs consider. One previously published "working typology" of ethical systems which bears relevance for a study of moral issues in criminal justice consists of three general "levels," with important subdivisions. It is as follows:

MACRO-ETHICS

Existential Ethics: values and beliefs relative to social behavior which derive from conceptual systems which transcend the mundane. Religious belief, deeply felt convictions about the significance of events, and understandings of the individual's purpose in life constitute the basis for existential ethics.

Ethics in Social Justice: the belief that certain social arrangements, especially between the weak and the powerful, the government and its citizens, or between and among social groups, should recognize moral imperatives.

Legal Ethics: the belief that our legal system and the laws which comprise it, are the embodiment of proper principles, and that the legal system itself is the result of moral struggle through a democratic process and therefore deserving of reverence and support.

MID-LEVEL ETHICS

Ethics in Criminal Justice: the belief that the processing of criminal defendants, the determination of guilt or innocence, and the treatment of convicted offenders, should adhere to socially acceptable standards of fairness.

Ethics in Professionalism: the belief that any profession, especially one which serves social ends, has an inherent worth which can be corrupted through inattention to precepts of propriety, and through the misguided behavior of individual members of that profession.

MICRO-ETHICS

On-the-Job Ethics: the belief, shared by members of a profession, that obligations toward one's fellow workers encompass duties and responsibilities, many of which are not always recognized by those outside the profession.

Personal Ethics: the beliefs and values acquired through the peculiarities of life and early socialization, including those learned from ethnic group participation, socialization into gender-specific roles, family routines, etc.[9]

Of no little significance to any consideration of criminal justice ethics is the fact that ethical messages sometimes conflict. Any or all of the seven ideational sources of ethics identified above can be active in the mind of a person faced with making an ethical decision of relevance to the criminal justice system. As a consequence, this bibliography contains materials which deal with each of these seven ethical wellsprings, even though most of our sources fall under the heading of "mid-level" ethics.

NOTES

(1) Prohibition, enacted with the 18th Amendment to the U.S. Consitution, became effective on January 29, 1919.

(2) Officially known as the National Commission of Law Observance and Enforcement.

(3) See, for example, Joseph J. Senna and Larry J. Siegel, **Introduction to Criminal Justice,** 5ed (St. Paul, MN: West Publishing Co., 1990) p. 4.

(4) National Advisory Commission on Criminal Justice Standards and Goals, **Police** (Washington, D.C.: U.S. Government Printing Office, 1973), p. 493.

(5) Knapp Commission, **Report on Police Corruption** (New York: George Braziller, 1973).

(6) A less elaborate version of these issues can be found in: Frank Schmalleger, **Ethics in Criminal Justice** (Bristol, IN: Wyndham Hall Press, 1990).

(7) Ibid., p. 2.

(8) The Law Enforcement Code of Ethics is promulgated primarily by the International Association of Chiefs of Police, Arlington, VA.

(9) **Ethics in Criminal Justice**, op. cit.

1
General Criminal Justice Policy and Law

1. Braswell, M. C., McCarthy, B. M., & McCarthy, B. J. (1991). **Justice, Crime and Ethics**. Cincinnati, OH: Anderson Publishing Co., 415 p.

> This anthology examines ethical dilemmas pertaining to professional activities in criminal justice and to criminal justice administration. A survey of philosophical perspectives on ethics is provided which contrasts the conflict between community interests and individual rights. The book covers policing, the courts, corrections, criminal justice research, and ethics and crime control policy. New philosophical models which might serve as future paradigms for workers in the criminal justice field are suggested. Numerous footnotes follow each contribution.

2. Elliston, F., & Bowie, N. (1982). **Ethics, Public Policy, and Criminal Justice**. Cambridge, MA: Oelgeschlager, Gunn & Hain, 483 p. NOTE: Some papers in this volume were originally presented at the conference "Ethics, Public Policy, and Criminal Justice" held at the University of Delaware in 1980.

> Twenty-three articles in this edited volume focus on defining crime, police morality and power, the ethics of punishment, judicial philosophy, and criminal justice policy. The ethical issues inherent in capital punishment and prisoner rights are explored, as are the ideology and ethics of white collar and other economic forms of crime. Separate author and subject indexes, along with a 24 page topical bibliography are provided.

3. Inciardi, J. A. (1990). **The Drug Legalization Debate**. Newbury Park, CA: Sage Publications, 264 p.

> This edited volume focuses on the problems which arise form the fact that the vigorous and expensive prosecution of drug users and dealers has not led to a noticeable reduction in drug use nor decreased the availability of controlled substances. The effectiveness of various forms of enforcement, as well as arguments for legalization, are considered. The legal and ethical dilemmas of the "war on drugs," the decriminalization of marijuana, and hidden paradigms in morality are discussed. NOTE: Portions were originally published as a special issue in **American Behavioral Scientist**, 32 (3).

4. Malloy, E. A. (1982). **Ethics of Law Enforcement and Criminal Punishment**. Lanham, MD: University Press of America, 99 p.

> This small volume focuses on ethics and the use of force by the police, police corruption, the ethical rationale for imprisonment, and capital punishment in the face of widespread public fear of violent crime. The author maintains that the professionalization model of police work in America should be implemented as quickly and extensively as possible. This will require significant efforts at upgrading recruitment activities, training practices, pay scales, command structures, and occupational self-definitions. In order to use discretion to serve the common good, police decision making must be informed by ethical principles that are defensible in the public forum. This book provides 106 footnotes.

5. National Center for Computer Crime Data. (1986). **Computer Crime, Computer Security, Computer Ethics: First Annual Statistical Report of the National Center for Computer Crime Data**. Los Angeles, CA: National Center for Computer Crime Data Publications, 34 p.

> Sixty-five graphs and tables are used to illustrate the seriousness of computer crimes in today's society. The majority of the graphs rely on data that was collected throughout 1985 and projected for 1986. Model state computer laws are discussed and ethical considerations are outlined for system users. The international aspects of computer crimes are detailed and relevant case law is reviewed. A resource guide is provided.

6. National Council on Crime and Delinquency. (1984). *Research and Criminal Justice Policy*. **Crime and Delinquency**, 30 (2), San

Francisco: National Council on Crime and Delinquency, 161 p.
NOTE: Complete volume.

This series of papers focuses on the link between research and criminal justice practice. Topics include the
ethics of selective incapacitation, the identification of
habitual offenders, using criminal intent as a measure of
crime seriousness, treatment and the role of classification, clinical sociology, correctional counseling, patterns
in juvenile misbehavior, and the advantages and dangers of juvenile diversion programs. Chapter references
and notes are provided.

7. Nettler, G. (1989). **Criminology Lessons: Arguments About
Crime, Punishment and the Interpretation of Conduct with Advice
for Individuals and Prescriptions for Public Policy.** Cincinnati,
OH: Anderson Publishing Company, 351 p.

This text provides lessons on the science of criminology,
using vignettes to illustrate major ethical, legal, social,
and   economic issues, as well as the notion of causation.
Chapters examine these issues with respect to individual
behavior, personal responsibility, larceny, embezzle-
ment, organized crime, disputes born of love relationships, and the dialectic which emerges from the strain
between calls for revenge and justice. The book concludes that mixed motives for inventing and applying
criminal law contribute to a criminal justice system that
is less than   rational, and that - in the arena where
public policy is formed - morality   wrestles with ration-
ality. Chapter notes and subject and name indexes are
provided.

8. Onder, J. (1976). **Maintaining Municipal Integrity.** Washington, D.C.: U.S. Department of Justice, National Institute of
Justice. NOTE: Videocassette, 47 minutes, color, 3/4 inch.

Government officials confront ethical dilemmas everyday. This videotape shows how some municipalities
have managed to overcome or prevent corruption. The
tape suggests that to sustain a noncorrupt government,
three elements are essential: prevention, maintenance,
and enforcement. Prevention entails a proactive approach involving codes, standards, and expectations.
Maintenance requires ethical standards, auditing procedures, and accountability. Enforcement involves punishment of those found guilty of engaging in corrupt
practices. These approaches are illustrated via discussion of representative governments in Illinois, Califor-

nia, and Colorado.

9. Pollock-Byrne, J. M. (1989). **Ethics in Crime and Justice: Dilemmas and Decisions**. Pacific Grove, CA: Brooks/Cole Publishing Company, 182 p.

The author reviews critical ethical issues facing the police, courts, and correctional subsystems of the justice system. She supplies workable definitions of ethics and morality while reviewing psychological theories of moral development. Relationships between society and various systems of government are discussed. Exemplary moral dilemmas are presented with accompanying ethical decision-making guidelines. An index and approximately 150 references are included.

10. Pring, R. K. (1988). *Logic and Values: A Description of a New Course in Criminal Justice and Ethics.* **The Justice Professional**, 3 (1), 94-106.

Herkimer County (New York) Community College offers a one credit hour course in "Ethics and Criminal Justice." The purpose of the course is to familiarize students with ethics and ethical decision making. Included are: moral logic, value analysis and clarification, and the making of moral decisions. Student response to the course is described, and progress in student ethical decision-making abilities is discussed.

11. Rather, R. S., et al. (1983). *Ethics in Criminological Research.* **Canadian Criminology Forum**, 6 (1), 61-74.

The author maintains that funding agencies in Canadian criminological research rely on ethical guidelines to disqualify research which may be perceived as threatening to the funding sources. Unfortunately for Canadian criminology research, the government has maintained a manipulative power that allows it to disqualify anyone who questions official government policy. The foibles of government agencies remain protected by the manner in which research is funded. A true picture of Canadian criminology will only develop when research is funded by parties that do not maintain a closely vested interest in the results.

12.   Schmalleger, F. A. (1990). **Ethics in Criminal Justice: A Justice Professional Reader**. Bristol, IN: Wyndham Hall Press, 218 p.

This collection of twelve articles from previous issues of

The Justice Professional covers the ethics of public defense, police professionalism, private security, and criminal defense in general. A number of the articles deal specifically with teaching ethics to criminal justice students, and with techniques for inculcating moral values. A typology of ethical concerns is included, along with a 23 page bibliography which lists hundreds of sources. Numerous endnotes follow each article.

13. Schmalleger, F. A., & Gustafson, R., (1981). **The Social Basis of Criminal Justice-Ethical Issues for the 1980's.** Washington, D.C.: University Press of America, 321 p.

The editors present a series of essays which identify ethical dilemmas that police, court, and correctional officials must face on a daily basis. These dilemmas include: personal and professional risks, prosecutorial discretion, professional standards as they relate to criminal trials, and the ethics of plea bargaining. The editors maintain that while there is a general concern with the standardization of ethical decision-making in these areas, there is no generally accepted international code of ethics applicable to criminal justice agencies or practices. The papers provide valuable suggestions for resolving many of these dilemmas.

14. Schmidt, D. P., & Victor, J. L. (1990). *Teaching Ethics in Criminal Justice.* In Roslyn Muraskin (ed.), **Issues in Justice: Exploring Policy Issues in the Criminal Justice System.** Bristol, IN: Wyndham Hall Press, 1990, 105-118.

Recognizing that ethical misconduct characterizes leaders in all segments of society, this paper advances a series of practical suggestions for teaching ethical concepts in a criminal justice university curriculum. The authors draw upon their own experience in discussing issues related to teaching, including: course content, questions of indoctrination, and the instructional process itself. Twelve endnotes are provided.

15. Shachar, Y. (1987). *The Fortuitous Gap in Law and Morality.* **Criminal Justice Ethics**, 6 (2), 12-36.

Building upon the observation that a person who attempts a crime but fails is often less seriously punished than one who successfully carries it out, the author maintains that a gap exists in the application of criminal law in most common law countries. Common conceptions of morality are said to provide the basis for this gap, and the nature of typical moral judgments is outlined. The author contrasts the writings of J. Piaget, concerning the moral development of children, with the evidence gathered by criminologists on adult understandings of crime severity. The article concludes that legal education seems to contribute nothing to the quality and content of moral judgments concerning crime. 160 footnotes are provided.

16. Sherman, L. W. (1982). **Ethics in Criminal Justice Education.** Hastings-on-Hudson, NY: The Hastings Center, 84 p.

This small book details the need for ethics in criminal justice, and outlines the historical development of ethical conceptions. The role of moral imagination, the morality of coercion, and technical and moral competence are discussed. Examples of adapting ethics to the criminal justice curriculum, issues of timing in the teaching of ethics, and ethics in research are considered. Professional codes of ethics are described. A bibliography and an appendix which provides addresses of professional agencies who have promulgated ethical codes are provided.

17. Smith, A. B. (1990). *Ethics of Criminological Research with Children as Subjects.* In Roslyn Muraskin (ed.), **Issues in Justice.** Bristol, IN: Wyndham Hall Press, 132-139.

This article takes issue with criminological researchers who may unintentionally stigmatize young children through research activities. Children are perceived as highly impressionable individuals who may be adversely affected by the labels peers and others apply to research subjects. Worse still are studies which identify future delinquents or career offenders when they are still in their teen years. Thirteen endnotes are listed.

18. Souryal, S. S. (1991). **Ethics in Criminal Justice.** Cincinnati, OH: Anderson Publishing Co. NOTE: forthcoming.

A thorough study of the classical roots of ethical theory, with relevance to the contemporary study of criminal justice. The author highlights the central role of moral choices within the administration of justice system, and stresses the role of moral judgment in enhancing the civility of criminal justice management. The book charges that the modern practice of criminal justice is more concerned with fighting crime than with doing justice, and stresses the need to introduce criminal justice students and practitioners to ethical thought.

19. United Nations. (1985). **Formulation and Application of United Nations Standards and Norms in Criminal Justice.** New York, NY: United Nations Publications, 24 p.

Since its foundation, the United Nations has played a crucial role in the formulation of criminal justice standards and norms. Standards have been developed for the treatment of prisoners and for the conduct of law enforcement officials. International initiatives are underway to implement these standards and to identify obstacles to effective implementation. Areas of interest for the development of new standards include alternatives to imprisonment, social resettlement of offenders, independence of the legal profession, the proper role of prosecutors, prisoners' rights, supervision of conditionally sentenced or released offenders, and the jurisdictional transfer of criminal proceedings. Major impediments to the effective application of standards and norms include poor coordination, a lack of funds, and public apathy. Increased intergovernmental, regional, and international cooperation is recommended to facilitate the implementation of United Nations standards. 15 footnotes are listed.

20. Wilbanks, W. (1987). **The Myth of a Racist Criminal Justice System.** Belmont, CA: Wadsworth, 209 p.

This book provides a lively critique of existing literature which concerns racial discrimination in the American system of criminal justice. The author, cognizant of differing perceptions between many black and white citizens, argues that although isolated cases of discrimination do occur, the system as a whole is generally fair and lacking in systematic bias. 700 item bibliography, 450 notes.

21. Wolfgang, M. E. (1981). *Confidentiality in Criminological Research and Other Ethical Issues.* **Journal of Criminal Law and Criminology,** 27 (1), 345-361. NOTE: An earlier version of this paper was presented at the Conference on Ethics, Public Policy and Criminal Justice, Center for the Study of Values, University of Delaware, Newark, Delaware, October 23-25, 1980.

Ethical issues associated with confidentiality in criminological research, the issuance of public or social policy statements, evaluation research, the use of research funds, and the teaching of criminology are discussed.

Topics selected for discussion center around the fact that criminological research frequently involves obtaining data from persons who could be criminally prosecuted based on the information they give to researchers. The author suggests that although researchers may not be legally immune from revealing their sources and producing confidential research information, the ethical commitment of the researcher should be to those who have provided data while working with the understanding that no adverse consequences would attend their participation. In sponsored research the researcher should be particularly careful that study findings are not slanted to cater to the self-interest of the sponsor. In teaching criminology, it is the obligation of the teacher to make clear to students particular biases that influence the perspectives the teacher presents in class. Footnotes are provided.

2
The Police

22. Abel, G. G., et al. (1986). *Sexually Aggressive Behavior.* In Curran, William J., et al. (eds.), **Forensic Psychiatry and Psychology**. Philadelphia, PA: F.A. Davis Company, 25 p.

Sexual assault is reviewed and a classification system is devised for sexually aggressive men. Current techniques of psychophysiological assessment, their implications for criminal justice purposes and ethical issues that these techniques might face are also discussed. Three categories of offenders are discussed. They are: the psychotic, those whose sexual offenses are incidental to other crimes, and the paraphiliac. Treatments are suggested for each category. Forty-six references are provided.

23. American Psychological Association. (1980). **Who Is the Client? The Ethics of Psychological Intervention in the Criminal Justice System**. Washington, D.C.: American Psychological Association, 174 p.

See Chapter 4, Corrections.

24. Benson, B. L., et al. (1988). *Doughnut Shop Ethics: There Are Answers.* **Police Chief**, 55 (12), 32-33.

The ethical dilemma of police gratuities, such as vendors offering free or reduced prices on items, provides the focus for this paper. Such conduct is said to be unprofessional and disliked by citizens. The potential for greater corruption is discussed. The author suggests that rules should be established and officers should be trained to properly handle situations involving proffered gratuities.

25. Bergstrom, K. R. (1985). *Police Experimentation With Civilian Subjects: Formalizing the Informal.* In Geller, William A. (ed.), **Police Leadership in America**. New York, NY: Praeger, 444-448.

This paper reviews several of the basic problems in police program experiments. Programs are said to often be justified simply on the questionable principle that measures morality according to whether benefits outweigh harms. Performing police experiments in one location simply because they were performed in another is said to ignore the reason why the experiment was conducted in the first place. The author suggests that unless there is a significant institutional interest involved, there may be no reason to conduct any experiment. It is pointed out that the results of an otherwise acceptable experiment may be ethically void if officers are pressured into participation against their personal judgment.

26. Biasotti, A. A. (1984). *Role of the Forensic Scientist in the Application of Chemical Tests for Alcohol in Traffic Law Enforcement.* **Journal of Forensic Sciences**, 29 (4), 1164-1172.

The role and ethical responsibilities of the forensic scientist are reviewed within the context of alcohol related traffic accidents. The mutual understanding of these responsibilities will assure cooperation among members of the criminal justice system who become involved in these circumstances. The suggested scientific validity of breath, blood, and urine tests for alcohol are presented.

27. Brady, J. B. (1983). *Justifiability of Hollow-Point Bullets.* **Criminal Justice Ethics**, 2 (2), 9-18.

Using the hollow-point bullet as an example, the issue of the appropriateness of police weapon systems is examined. The decision of one police department to adopt the hollow-point bullet has led to a close reexamination of what issues are relevant when making this sort of decision. Issues include: police-community relations, police morale, official policy, and use of deadly force when adequate backup is not available. Specific equipment issues which are discussed include: accuracy of the round, stopping power, ricocheting, and wounding effects of the round. A total of 22 notes are provided.

28. Canadian Author (Unk). (1981). **Organizational Police Deviance: Its Structure and Control.** Scarborough, Ontario: Butterworth Company, 213 p.

The goal of furthering practical law enforcement objectives leads Canadian researchers to the discovery of abuses in policing. The fact that extra-legal factors influence police decision-making is reviewed. Organizational deviance is found difficult to control when many decisions rest on extra-legal factors.

29. Cohen, H. (1985). *Dilemma for Discretion.* In Heffernan, William C., et al. (eds.), **Police Ethics: Hard Choices in Law Enforcement.** New York, NY: John Jay Press, 69-80.

The author argues that police officers must be trained in moral reasoning so they may properly exercise the discretion which is naturally theirs. The peacekeeping and social service functions of police officers are discussed. It is suggested that the police should be permitted to keep the peace and provide social services without strict and formal enforcement of all laws, provided (1) the means they employ for achieving those ends are reasonable, (2) the least offensive means are used to achieve these ends, and (3) the means do not subvert another end of equal or greater importance. Eleven notes are provided.

30. _____. (1987). *Overstepping Police Authority*, **Criminal Justice Ethics** 6 (2), 52-60.

The author explores the dimensions of police authority, with an eye toward how that authority is defined - both by individual practitioners and society in general. Because police authority is both highly specific (defined by law) and exceedingly vague (in the face of specific instances of enforcement) the ethics of police work are difficult to define. The interpretation that an officer gives to a situation may vary considerably from the interpretation society places upon that same situation. The question then becomes not only one of how to act, but of whether or not significant social and personal consequences will attach to any discretionary decision. Nine footnotes.

31. D'Agostino, C. (1986). *Police Psychological Services: Ethical Issues.* In Goldstein, et al. (eds.), **Psychological Services for Law Enforcement.** Rockville, MD: U.S. Department of Justice, Federal Bureau of Investigation, 241-247.

This paper presents ethical issues that should be considered by police psychologists and their employers. Issues include: responsibilities, competence, moral and legal standards, public statements, confidentiality, the welfare of the officer/client, professional relationships, and assessment techniques. A series of strategies are provided to assist in the development of ethical guidelines for police psychologists. Eleven references are provided.

32. Delaney, H. R. (1988). *Toward a Police Professional Ethic.* **The Justice Professional**, 3 (1), 39-55.

An important moral requirement facing those within the current movement to professionalize the police is the development of a general ethical position that defines the nature of the relationship between the police and the general public. This paper contends that police professional conduct should be grounded in a sense of the virtues, i.e., those traits of character that will serve stated purposes in the police occupational role. The virtues are said to include a sense of justice as equality, and a sense of retribution as the operative rationale for the justification of punishment.

33. Delattre, E. J. (1989). **Character and Cops: Ethics in Policing**. Lanham, MD: University Press of America, 264 p.

The author examines the ethical standards of the police profession, from those which apply to department heads, to officers on the beat. He argues that ethical behavior is crucial for the success of police activities and for the survival of American society. Discretion, corruption, authority, and leadership are all explored within the context of moral character. Character training and development are considered and education in moral problem solving is described. The potential for corruption associated with narcotics enforcement is detailed in a separate chapter. An index is provided.

34. Dougherty, A. N. (1986). *Drug Testing: America's New Work Ethic?* **Stetson Law Review**, 15 (3), 883-913.

The legal case of the *City of Palm Bay v. Bauman,* gave credence to the fact that police officers are no different than many other federal and local government employees who are being subjected to drug testing. While the court did protect individuals from random drug tests, it clearly stated that those suspected of drug use (on or off duty) were susceptible to drug testing. The author suggests that this is yet another small cut at the Fourth Amendment's ability to protect the individual from the whims of an employer's perceived need to know. 202 footnotes are provided.

35. Doyle, J. F. (1985). *Police Discretion, Legality and Morality.* In Heffernan, William C., et al. (eds.), **Police Ethics: Hard Choices in Law Enforcement,** New York, NY: John Jay Press, 47-68.

This paper examines whether police discretion can be reconciled with requirements of legality and morality. Police often have strong discretionary powers and are free to make official choices without being effectively subject to independent standards for such choices. In reconciling police discretion with legality, the author suggests, police must appreciate the limits of legal rulemaking and rule compliance, since these limits explain why discretion is necessary. Thirty-seven notes are provided.

36. Elliston, F. A. (Unk). **Deadly Force: An Ethical Analysis.** Albany, NY: Hindelang Criminal Justice Research Center.

The author maintains that a review of available literature on capital punishment is critical in identifying moral factors which should be considered when developing defensible policies for police officers confronted with the decision of whether or not to use deadly force. The author suggests that moral issues surrounding capital punishment also apply to the deadly force dilemma. Six elements in the use of deadly force are discussed: social defense, justice, the sanctity of human life, fallibility or irrevocability, due process, and contemporary moral standards. Includes 21 references.

37. ____. (1985). *Deadly Force and Capital Punishment: A Comparative Appraisal.* In Heffernan, William C., et al. (eds.), **Police Ethics - Hard Choices in Law Enforcement,** New York, NY: John Jay Press, 513-167.

The author maintains that the legal and ethical reasoning which supports arguments both for and against capital punishment has direct implications for police policies dealing with the use of deadly force. Just as pro-capital punishment individuals would apply a balancing test to individual cases, the same test may be applied to the issue of deadly force. However, the issue of capital punishment is a planned procedure, and while one may plan on using deadly force some day, the incident is often a momentary decision by one individual. 29 notes are provided.

38. Elliston, F. A., & Feldberg, M. (1985). **Moral Issues in Police Work.** Totowa, NJ: Rowan and Allanheld Publishers, 304 p.

A series of fifteen essays on ethical issues in policing are presented. Essay topics include: authority, discretion, police function, deception as an investigative technique, the use of force, and police corruption. Four of the essays discuss ethical rationales for police use of force in a society dedicated to peace. Chapter notes, a 72-item bibliography, and a subject index are provided.

39. Felkenes, G. T. (1984). *Attitudes of Police Officers Toward Their Professional Ethics.* **Journal of Criminal Justice,** 12 (3), 211-220.

This study investigates how police officers in several police agencies view their professional ethics. Police officers are faced with a maze of obligations in the performance of their official duties. The 'Law Enforcement Code of Ethics' and 'Canons of Police Ethics' were created to make explicit the conduct considered appropriate for police officers and to guide them in the performance of their duties. However, this study indicates that individual officers rely on personal ethics in situations where standard official ethics are not clear, and suggests a need for further research into the application of police ethics.

40. Graybosch, A. J. (1985). *Proactive Patrol, Privacy, and Target Selection.* **The Justice Professional,** 1 (1), 14-25.

Legal and ethical issues in policing while using proactive patrol strategies are discussed. Proactive patrol strategies have proven to be quite effective against white-collar criminals and recidivists. However, an individual's moral, social and legal right to privacy are endangered by the nature of proactive patrol. Undercover operations are said to border on entrapment because of their specific enticement of preselected individuals. The extent to which society is willing to tolerate such police actions is explored. Thirty footnotes are included.

41. Green, C. J. C. (1985). *The Ethics of Protest.* **Police Journal,** 58 (1), 17-21.

This essay discusses the effects of policing when it takes the form of military occupation and has less than consensus support from the civilian sector. The discussion centers on the military type policing that is said to exist in the inner city areas of mainland Britain. This type of policing may not represent the best interests of all citizens yet the government views it as necessary.

42. Hansen, D. A. (1973). **Police Ethics**. Springfield, IL: Charles C. Thomas, 78 p.

This small volume centers around a discussion of the *Law Enforcement Code of Ethics.* The term "ethics" is defined and made applicable to police work, and the concept of police professionalism is detailed. Examples of police immorality, including proffered gratuities and solicited improprieties, are described and discussed. Police administration is described within the context of discipline. A brief index is provided.

43. Heffernan, W. C. (1985). *Police and Their Rules of Office: An Ethical Analysis.* In Heffernan, William C., et al. (eds.), **Police Ethics - Hard Choices in Law Enforcement**, New York, NY: John Jay Press, 22 p.

This essay assesses police justifications for illegal searches and seizures, illegal stops and frisks, and selective law enforcement. The ethical and moral beliefs of the officer are examined under circumstances where he or she is given more than the usual degree of latitude in professional decision making. The author suggests that both statutes and departmental policies should be used to specify procedures for making discretionary decisions. Nineteen notes are included.

44. Heffernan, W. C., & Stroup, T. (1985). **Police Ethics: Hard Choices in Law Enforcement**. New York, NY: John Jay Press, 225 p. NOTE: papers taken from the conference "Police Ethics" held on April 22-25, 1982 at the Institute for Criminal Justice Ethics, John Jay College.

This is a collection of eleven papers which examine police discretion, whistle-blowing, undercover work, deceptive investigations, privacy, deadly force, affirmative action, and sexual integration in American law enforcement. A detailed index is provided.

45. International Association of Chiefs of Police. (1965). *Law Enforcement Code of Ethics.* Gaithersburg, MD: IACP, 1 p.

This is the standard version of the law enforcement code of ethics. It stresses the duty of law enforcement officers to serve the public, to safeguard lives and property, to protect the weak against oppression, to protect the peaceful against violence, and to respect the United States Constitution, and the rights guaranteed to individuals under the constitution.

46. International Association of Chiefs of Police Bureau of Operations and Research. (1980). **Police Ethics - Training Key Number 295**. Gaithersburg, MD: International Association of Chiefs of Police Publications, 6 p.

This training key for police officers covers duties under the law, relations with the public, and conflicts arising from a multilevel professional commitment. A canon of police ethics is included. A discussion guide, questions and answers, and one reference are provided.

47. Inwald, R. E. (1985). *Administrative, Legal, and Ethical Practices in the Psychological Testing of Law Enforcement Officers.* **Journal of Criminal Justice**, 13 (4), 367-372.

Legal and ethical issues surrounding the use of psychological testing on police applicants are discussed. Privacy, the validity of testing, racial and sexual biases in police hiring, and standards for suitable police candidates are described. The author suggests ten uniform guidelines on employee selection procedures as aids to assist law enforcement officials in making ethical decisions in hiring practices.

48. Jones, D. M. (1987). *Using the 'Unfinished Story' as a Mechanism for Exploring Ethical Dilemmas in Criminal Investigation.* **The Justice Professional**, 2 (2), 64-77.

This article describes one mechanism for dealing with ethical issues: 'the unfinished story.' This approach attempts to force the police student to resolve some of the dilemmas that may be inherent in certain elements of police work, while also developing writing skills. The strengths and pitfalls of such an approach are discussed. It is concluded that such an approach may well be worth considering by others who teach in the field.

49. Kania, R. R. E. (1988). *Should We Tell the Police to say 'Yes' to Gratuities?* **Criminal Justice Ethics**, 7 (2), 37-49.

The ethical impropriety of police accepting minor gratuities has been treated as an established fact, with only the degree of impropriety involved being subject to debate. It is argued that especially the police, and sometimes other justice officials, should be encouraged to accept freely offered minor gratuities. Such gratuities, rather than being perceived as incipient corruptors, should be viewed as the building blocks of positive social relationships between the police and the public. One table and 33 notes are provided.

50. Kelling, G. L. (1985). *Justifying the Moral Propriety of Experimentation: A Case Study.* In Geller, William A. (ed.), **Police Leadership in America**. New York, NY: Praeger Publishers, 6 p.

This paper reviews some of the ethical issues posed by the Kansas City Proactive Patrol Program. This experiment tested the effectiveness of proactive police patrol by withdrawing preventive patrol from randomly selected sections of the city without informing residents. Many officers and supervisors questioned the morality of depriving citizens of police patrol without their consent or knowledge. Crime statistics were monitored weekly in the unpatrolled areas and promises were made that the experiment would be terminated if the crime rates in these locales were to markedly increase.

51. Krajick, K. (1980). *Police vs. Police - No One Knows Much About Internal Affairs Bureaus, So Everyone Distrusts Them.* **Police Magazine**, 3 (3), 6-15, 17-20.

This article examines the operation of police internal affairs units in several major cities. Officers coming under scrutiny from these review boards often complain of personal grudges, whims, and politics. It has been suggested by some writers that criminals have more rights in the judicial system than officers do before a review board. Inconsistencies in police review boards have brought sharp criticism from fraternal police organizations and unions.

52. LeClere, M. (1982). *Police Ethics and Conduct.* **International Criminal Police Review**, (358), 122-131.

This paper assesses the United Nations Code of Conduct for law enforcement officials, which advocates public protection, respect for human rights, the ensuring of confidentiality, and refraining from corruption. Issues not mentioned by the Code are raised by the author. Areas requiring further clarification and definition are presented. The complete United Nations Code of Conduct for law enforcement officials is appended.

53. McCarthy, R. (1988). *Real Issues and Answers on Police Use of Deadly Force.* **Police Chief,** 55 (10), 33-37.

Police agencies should take proactive steps to ensure that, when and if an officer has to use deadly force they can do so appropriately, professionally and consistently within acceptable laws, policies, procedures and ethics. Prior to an occurrence, police agencies should have a preplanned strategy to handle public controversies and crises which often arise under such circumstances. Proper police preparation would include fact finding instruments which show both the positive and negative issues surrounding various elements in the use of deadly force.

54. Marx, G.T. (1985). *Police Undercover Work: Ethical Deception of Deceptive Ethics?* In Heffernan, William C., et al. (eds.), **Police Ethics: Hard Choices in Law Enforcement.** New York, NY: John Jay Press, 83-115.

The author presents a checklist of questions to help assess the appropriateness of legal and ethical decisions regarding undercover activity. The checklist represents a mental recollection of all the facts and circumstances surrounding a particular undercover operation. It is suggested that while each point on the list does not have to stand alone on its own merit, the cumulative checklist should determine the appropriateness of an undercover operation. 48 notes are provided.

55. ___. (1988). **Undercover: Police Surveillance in America.** Berkeley, CA: University of California Press, 309 p.

A variety of undercover-type operations and related ethical issues are discussed. Sources for this study include: official records, unpublished documents, and interviews with the Federal Bureau of Investigation and local California police agencies. An analysis of the goals, nature, targets, and techniques of undercover and surveillance operations suggests changes which have occurred over time. Some of intended and unintended consequences of covert operations are considered.

Notable are unintended breaches of individuals' rights to privacy and consent. The ethical aspects of decisions made by those conducting undercover surveillance are analyzed.

56. Massachusetts State Ethics Commission. (1986). **Chiefs of Police Doing Privately Paid Details: Commission Advisory No. 10.** Boston, MA: Massachusetts State Publications, 4 p.

This advisory by the Massachusetts State Ethics Commission specifies those circumstances under which small-town police chiefs may be paid for off-duty work without violating state conflict-of-interest laws. The advisory explains how a police chief's employment arrangement can be restructured so as to avoid conflict of interest violations. Six footnotes are provided.

57. Metz, H. W. (1986). *An Ethical Model for Law Enforcement Administrators.* **The Justice Professional,** 1 (2), 72-77.

This article deals with the ethical concerns of police administrators and officers in this post-Watergate age. The officer's moral career, as it is linked with the administrator's ability to foster conditions which enhance ethical conduct, is described. Specific actions that can be undertaken by administrators interested in ethical conduct are documented.

58. More, H. W., & Shipley, O. R. (1987). **Police Policy Manual: Personnel.** Springfield, IL: Charles C. Thomas, 259 p.

This book is intended to serve as a reference for appropriate policies and procedures for small police agencies. Guidance is provided in the following areas: administration, ethical standards, working conditions, personnel management, personnel development, internal investigations, and the use of deadly force. Ethical standards which are provided include guidelines and rights that should be afforded to police officers as well as citizens. The various aspects of running a functioning police department are discussed. Sample forms are provided.

59. Muir, W. K. (1983). *Police and Politics.* **Criminal Justice Ethics,** 2 (2), 3-9.

The author discusses some of the modern arguments against police activity in politics and suggests benefits that may result from their participation. All discussions center on the three police goals of: improved police ethics, enhanced public understanding, and improved public policy. Seven advantages are cited as resulting from police entering in the electoral process. Close supervision by internal review boards and journalist organizations are said to be essential to preventing police corruption of this opportunity. Four notes are supplied.

60. ___. (1985). *Should Police Participate Actively in Electoral Politics?* In Heffernan, William C., et al. (eds.), **Police Ethics: Hard Choices in Law Enforcement.** New York, NY: John Jay Press, 171-181.

The author argues that the benefits of police participation in the electoral process outweigh the disadvantages, and offers various means for preventing the corruption of the process. The arguments against police participation include suggestions that it: (1) is unnecessary since police clientele are typically criminal offenders, (2) undermines public perceptions of police neutrality, and (3) is a direct threat to the democratic process. Positive arguments cite: (1) a balancing of interest groups, (2) education of the public, (3) improved public debate, (4) enhanced police leadership responsibilities, (5) a heightened awareness of police residency, (6) the enhancement of police communications skills, and (7) a decrease in distrust of the police. Three notes are provided.

61. Muscari, P. G. (1984). *Police Corruption and Organizational Structures: An Ethicist's View.* **Journal of Criminal Justice,** 12 (3), 235-245.

Structural explanations have provided social scientists with a penetrating look at the dynamic and interactional forces that bear upon human behavior. This has been especially revealing in criminal justice where such an approach has quite dramatically shown that corrupt practices arise through the evolution of a problematic infrastructure within police departments. By taking a radical departure from current orthodoxy, this paper argues that structural explanation has its place in a discussion of human behavior. When overextended, however, as the author suggests it has been in the present literature on police corruption, it reaches unsound theoretical conclusions that neglect the self and express a disdain for the personal - all of which runs counter to the development of useful ethical standards.

62. Onder, J. (Unk). **Maintaining Municipal Integrity**. Washington, D.C.: Department of Justice, National Institute of Justice. NOTE: Videocassette, 47 minutes, color, 3/4 inch.

This video tape describes how government officials come to confront ethical dilemmas on a daily basis and shows how some municipalities overcame and prevented corruption. Corruption warning signs as well as steps that can be taken to prevent corruption are discussed. One of the first steps presented includes the development of laws, policies, codes, standards, and expectations for all employees. Maintenance and reactive steps are also discussed. Several approaches to corruption are illustrated by the governments of Arlington Heights, IL, San Diego, CA, and Colorado Springs, CO.

63. Payton, G. T. (1982). **Patrol Procedure and Enforcement Concepts**. Los Angeles, CA: Legal Book Corporation, 580 p.

This textbook covers aspects of police patrol ranging from ethical concerns to record keeping, criminal identification, interrogation, and the handling of emergency calls. An analysis of the Law Enforcement Code of Ethics emphasizes how field officers can translate the code into practice. This book identifies the types of patrol used by modern police departments and provides guidance for the various tasks and duties that a police officer may be required to preform. Photographs, diagrams, and references accompany each chapter. An index is provided.

64. Peterson, J. (1984). *Promises, Compromises, and Commitments.* **American Behavioral Scientist**, 27 (4), 453-480.

A review of the scientific, legal, fiscal, and political forces that are contributing to the growth of state and local forensic laboratories is provided. Ethical issues that arose during a government-funded study of the methods and accuracy of crime laboratories in analyzing standard forms of physical evidence are discussed. The issue of confidentiality is also examined. Thirty-six references are provided.

65. The President's Commission on Law Enforcement and Administration of Justice. (1967). **Task Force Report: The Police.** Washington, D.C.: U.S. Gov't. Printing Office, 668 p.

This is one in a series of reports prepared by the President's Commission on Law Enforcement and Administration of Justice. *The Police* provides a general overview of police services in America in the late 1960's while paying special attention to the problems of policing a free society. Chapter 7 of the report is entitled "Police Integrity" and deals generally with ethical issues. Methods for maintaining integrity in law enforcement are discussed, including personnel selection, training, internal investigations, and the vigorous prosecution of cases of dishonesty. Although dated, this report is of special historical significance because it drew national attention to ethical issues at a time when police improvements were viewed primarily in terms of technology and crime-fighting ability.

66. Price, B. R. (1985). *Sexual Integration in American Law Enforcement.* In Heffernan, William C., et al. (eds.), **Police Ethics: Hard Choices in Law Enforcement**. New York, NY: John Jay Press, 205-218.

The author maintains that the low representation of women in policing is partially due to stereotyped images of police officers and departmental opportunities for hiring and advancement. Women are necessary in policing to add a diversity of opinion and representation. Factually speaking, more women are being accepted into departments today than was the case ten years ago. However, the majority of these women are at entry-level supervisory positions or lower. Other factors that effect the disproportionate representation of women in policing are discussed. Twenty-three notes are provided.

67. Schmalleger, F. (1988). *Police Ethics: A Teaching Bibliography.* **The Justice Professional**, 3 (1), 171-178.

This ethics bibliography serves to increase the availability of important materials within the criminal justice profession. Included in this bibliography are sources which clearly and directly focus upon ethics and the police, while simultaneously holding value for classroom instruction. The bibliography is limited to a 15-year period, going back no farther in the literature than 1972, unless the piece in question was truly 'historic' (formed the basis for a number of future discourses). The areas of corrections, law, and the courts are omitted with plans to publish them at a later date.

68. Schroeder, O. C. (1984). *Ethical and Moral Dilemmas Confronting Forensic Scientists.* **Journal of Forensic Sciences**, 29 (4),

966-986.

Forensic scientists are often caught in moral dilemmas that represent a "no win" situation. Due to the diverse roles of forensic scientists -- as chemists, physicians, criminalists, etc. -- there is ample opportunity for multiple interpretations of their reports and professional conclusions. As expert witnesses in the legislative, executive, and judicial arenas of law and justice it is becoming increasingly important that the ethics of forensic scientists be firmly established so as to minimize the opportunities for misinterpretation and misunderstanding.

69. Shapard, J. E. (1985). *Ethics of Experimentation in Law Enforcement.* In Geller, William A. (ed.), **Police Leadership in America.** New York, NY: Praeger, 418-429.

This paper outlines the conclusions of the Federal Judicial Center's Advisory Committee on Experimentation in the Law regarding the ethics of conducting justice system experiments. The ethical principles outlined in this paper apply to 'program' type experiments, which alter the operation of an existing component of the justice system. This usage of the term distinguishes "programs" from simulations or laboratory experiments. The committee's ethical guidance centered on the fact that decisions about program experiments are linked to justice system administrators' decisions about how their institutions ought to function. As a consequence, it is suggested, ethical considerations in experimentation must derive from the same ethics that guides all administrative decisions about institutional operations. Further guidance is given in the areas of: (1) providing needed information, (2) random assignment research, and (3) need-based improvement of the justice system. Five notes are provided.

70. Sherman, L. W. (1978). **The Quality of Police Education.** San Francisco, CA: Jossey-Bass.

This is a report by the National Advisory Commission on Higher Education for Police Officers. It contains an overview of programs on higher education for police officers as those programs existed in the late 1970's. The credentials of faculty members in criminal justice curricula, and the experiences of students studying in those programs are described. Recommendations are made for the improvement of police education. This report is significant because of its recognition of the value of ethics education. Recommendation 3-5 reads: *"Every police education program should include in its required curriculum a thorough consideration of the value choices and ethical dilemmas of police work."* (p. 4).

71. _____. (1982). *Learning Police Ethics.* **Criminal Justice Ethics,** 1 (1), 10-19.

New police officers develop their values from experiences on the street and from interaction with more experienced police officers. Traditional police values include such ideas as: (1) due process is only a means of protecting criminals at the expense of the law-abiding, and (2) lying and deception are an essential part of the police task. A total of 12 notes are provided.

72. ___. (1985). *Equity Against Truth: Value Choices in Deceptive Investigations.* In Heffernan, William C., et al. (eds.), **Police Ethics: Hard Choices in Law Enforcement.** New York, NY: John Jay Press, 117-132.

The author advocates deception in criminal investigations when the target is a white-collar criminal. However, randomness is presented as the only fair targeting method for undercover investigations. The current method of relying on informants and tips is said to be too easily abused by both criminals and investigators. Guidelines for defining a target population are provided with the caveat that they should adhere to constitutional rulings in connection with certain population groups. Thirteen notes are provided.

73. _____. (1987). *Reinventing Probable Cause: Target Selection in Proactive Investigations.* **Journal of Social Issues,** 43 (3), 87-94.

Probable cause is provided as a safeguard proposed in Braithwaite et al's (1987) defense of the use of covert facilitation for the detection of the white-collar criminal. Due to the difficulty in applying probable cause against a large unknown suspect pool, however, the author suggests that random or equal probability selection be applied to known suspects within a certain category. This, he suggests, could prove to be much more rewarding, as statistics demonstrate that a small number of suspects are responsible for the majority of crimes. Categorical probable cause is cited as contributing to more democratic policing. Nine references are provided.

74. Stroup, T. (1985). *Affirmative Action and the Police.* In Heffernan, William C., et al. (eds.), **Police Ethics: Hard Choices in Law Enforcement.** New York, NY: John Jay Press, 183-203.

The author states that ideal practices in police hiring should reward those candidates who possess personal qualifications which are likely to promote productivity and efficiency, yet stresses that affirmative action programs must be continuously taken into consideration in any hiring decision. According to the author, an equal balance should be achieved between qualifications and affirmative action requirements so that an environment infused with elements of both equality and opportunity can be created. Any hiring program that strictly relies on achievement is said to freeze in place the consequences and patterns of past hiring discrimination. Fifteen notes are provided.

75. United Nations. (1980). **Code of Conduct for Law Enforcement Officials.** New York, NY: United Nations Publications, 5 p.

A code of conduct for law enforcement officials, stating that those who exercise police powers shall respect and protect human dignity and uphold the human rights of all persons, was adopted by the United Nations General Assembly in December 1979. Governments are urged to consider using the Code in their framework of national legislation and practice. Commentary on each of the eight articles provides definitions and discusses the purpose of each.

76. ___. (1985). **Formulation and Application of United Nations Standards and Norms in Criminal Justice.** New York, NY: United Nations Publications, 24 p.

See Chapter 1, Policy and Law.

77. U.S. General Accounting Office. (1988). **Ethics Enforcement: Results of Conflict of Interest Investigations.** Washington, D.C.: U.S. General Accounting Office Publications, 18 p.

A review was conducted of alleged violations of criminal conflict of interest statutes reported to 10 agency Offices of the Inspector General (OIG's) during 1985 and 1986. From these sites, agencies had referred 124 allegations to the U.S. Department of Justice for prosecutive action. Of these, 112 involved conflicts of interest. Of the 124 allegations, one resulted in conviction, another is an open case. The Department declined to prosecute 107 of the referrals and has not decided whether to prosecute 13. Agencies took administrative action (e.g., suspension or dismissal) on 22 allegations, including 16 involving conflicts of interest. Supplemental survey forms and survey information are appended. Tables are included.

78. Weiner, B. A. (1986). *Confidentiality and the Legal Issues Raised By the Psychological Evaluations of Law Enforcement Officers.* In Goldstein, H. A., et al. (eds.), **Psychological Services for Law Enforcement.** Washington, D.C.: U.S. Department of Justice, Federal Bureau of Investigation, 97-102.

While the right to privileged communications does not apply to police candidates during psychological testing, there are personal rights and professional ethics that must be considered. An evaluation may not be discriminatory and must assess the candidate on job related psychological characteristics. Candidates must be aware of pending actions should the results of the testing be less than favorable. Ethically, the language utilized in the psychological report must be clear so as not to cause the reader to cast an unnecessary shadow of doubt on the results. Twenty-one footnotes are provided.

79. Wish, E. D. (1986). **Identification of Drug Abusing Offenders: A Guide for Practitioners**, Draft Report. Rockville, MD: National Institute of Justice, 25 p.

This draft report is intended to act as a guide for those criminal justice agencies that find it necessary to identify drug abusing offenders. The report discusses some of the reasons why it may be beneficial to criminal justice agencies to be aware of drug abusing offenders. Four methods of identifying drug abusing offenders are discussed. The legal and ethical ramifications of urinalysis tests are presented. Forty-nine references are provided.

80. Wren, T. E. (1985). *Whistle-Blowing and Loyalty to One's Friends.* In Heffernan, William C., et al. (eds.), **Police Ethics: Hard Choices in Law Enforcement.** New York, NY: John Jay Press, 25-43.

The moral dilemma facing police officers who observe minor professional misconduct among their peers is discussed. While the offending officers' actions may appear to be minor, the observing officers know that their reporting the observed discretions will certainly cause severe personal consequences for them. A sub-cultural ethic must be created which objectively views the immorality and social consequences of law enforcement corruption.

3
The Courts

81. American Bar Association. (1972). **Code of Judicial Conduct.** Chicago, IL: American Bar Association, Special Committee on Standards of Judicial Conduct, 32 p.

> This Code is a modification of the **Canons of Judicial Ethics** adopted by the ABA in 1924. The seven canons are enumerated and accompanying text material discusses the significance and applicability of each. A final section outlines the conditions under which compliance with the Code is expected.

82. American Psychological Association. (1980). **Who Is the Client? The Ethics of Psychological Intervention in the Criminal Justice System.** Washington, D.C.: American Psychological Association Publications, 174 p.

> *See Chapter 4, Corrections.*

83. Appelbaum, P. S. (1987). *In the Wake of* Ake: *The Ethics of Expert Testimony in an Advocate's World.* **Bulletin of the American Academy of Psychiatry and the Law,** 15 (1), 15-25.

> The decision of the U.S. Supreme Court in *Ake v. Oklahoma* redefined the role of psychiatrists as experts in criminal cases. In addition to the expert's serving as evaluator and witness, the Court emphasized the importance of the defense having a psychiatrist available to act as a consultant in the preparation and presentation of its case. This broader conception of the expert's role has raised ethical questions among psychiatrists, many of whom are concerned that their impartiality may be compromised. A careful analysis of *Ake,* however,

demonstrates that substantial differences remain between the roles of consultant and advocate. Several ethical issues related to the consultative role are considered and possible means of dealing with them addressed. Twelve references are provided.

84. Berger, B. J. (1983). *Prosecution's Rebuttal Argument: The Proper Limits of the Doctrine of 'Invited Response.'* **Criminal Law Bulletin**, 19 (1), 5-21.

This article deals primarily with the practical and ethical problems associated with the 'invited response' doctrine. The author finds that prosecutors too often unfairly use this doctrine in their rebuttal arguments and go far beyond the scope of defense counsels' closing arguments. Appellate courts, in the author's view, are too lenient with such prosecutors and have not developed a useful analytical approach to the problem. The author sets out his version of the proper analytical framework and gives helpful examples to test that framework in action.

85. Blanck, P. D. (1987). *The Process of Field Research in the Courtroom.* **Law and Human Behavior**, 11 (4), 337-358.

This article discusses the methodological and ethical issues the author faced in a courtroom research project on trial judges' verbal and nonverbal behavior in criminal jury trials. Only by studying judges while they presided over actual trials could the researcher both describe judicial behavior and determine the effect such behavior had on trial processes. Data collection techniques included field notes, courtroom questionnaires, interviewing, videotaping in the courtroom, and unobtrusive data collection techniques in the courtroom. Even after data were obtained and the researchers had withdrawn from the courtroom, issues of confidentiality, usefulness, and clearances persisted. 97 references.

86. Brakel, S. J. (1986). *Pro Se.* **Student Lawyer**, 14 (6), 38-40.

The author suggests that the public's view of lawyers as inordinately money-hungry is based upon an intuitive recognition of fact. A survey of publications for lawyers is said to demonstrate a strong monetary focus. The concept of self-interest is explored, and the need for better internal policing of the legal profession is stressed. Sanctions for frivolous suits are suggested, and advertising by suit-seeking lawyers is discouraged.

87. Brink, D. R. (1982). *The Image, the Truth, and the Bard.* **ABA Journal**, May, 1982, 510.

A past president of the American Bar Association expresses his view that lawyers are unfairly criticized for being unethical. The internal standards of the legal profession are stressed, as are the potential punishments imposed on errant practitioners. The divergence between public opinion and fact is discussed.

88. Brooks, T. J. (1984). *How Judges Get Into Trouble: Ethics and Discipline Today.* **Judges' Journal**, 23 (3), 4-7, 52-56.

The American Bar Association Model Code of Judicial Conduct serves as the basic national standard for judicial conduct and provides a basis for uniformity in judicial ethics. Adoptions of the code, or separate standards, by the states and the District of Columbia are explored. Case law involving misconduct on the bench, misconduct off the bench, and misconduct caused by disability is outlined. The field of judicial ethics is seen as evolving, with much agreement on the definition of misconduct, but less uniformity in the discipline process. Case illustrations, an annotated list of sources of information on judicial ethics, and 74 reference notes are supplied.

89. Burt, R. A. (1981). *Conflict and Trust Between Attorney and Client.* **Georgetown Law Journal**, 69 (4), 1015-1046.

This article argues that mistrust characterizes the relationship between attorneys and clients, and that practical incentives and formal norms of the legal profession lead attorneys and clients to resist admitting this mistrust. The impact of the American Bar Association's Model Rules of Professional Conduct on this situation is examined. The proposed rules mandate that certain attorney-client relationships begin with an explicit warning to clients of consequences potentially adverse to their interests if they reveal too much about themselves. However, these rules may add new incentives for resistance to disclosure of client communication and may exacerbate mistrust. Paradoxically, more stringent disclosure requirements might prompt honest exploration of attorney-client mistrust and might ultimately enhance trust in professional relations. The article includes 121 footnotes.

90. Chung, W. S., Edwards, D. W., & Roundtree, G. A. (1980). *Application of the Theory of Communicative Competence in the Analysis of Juror's Decision-Making Structure.* **International Journal of Comparative and Applied Criminal Justice**, 4 (1), 95-104.

This study aimed to ascertain whether or not presuppositions or value-laden data affect a juror's decision-making process. It applied the theory of communicative competence in analyzing the decision-making process in juries. Whether juries use a rational communicative structure was explored by examining the court transcript from a trial of a shoplifter and by conducting interviews with two jury members to determine whether the jurors' verdicts were based on universal truth and moral values. Questions are raised of how to improve the jury's decision-making structure. Ten references are provided.

91. Copple, R. F. (1988). *From the Cloister to the Street: Judicial Ethics and Public Expression.* **Denver University Law Review**, 64 (3), 549-578.

This examination of legal, ethical, and policy considerations regarding the public role of judges concludes that judicial participation in educating the public about the legal system far outweighs any illusory fears that such a role taints judicial objectivity. Given the lack of specificity about judicial expression in the official Code of Judicial Conduct, guidelines for judicial expression are shown to be best derived from a synthesis of the code and supporting materials. Such an analysis indicates that as a public servant, a judge has a duty to help educate the public. Judges are in a position to view the law from an objective and impartial perspective, so judges, of all public officials, may be the best qualified to perform the task of educating the public about the law and the legal system. This means, however, that judges must be willing to expose themselves to criticism when they comment on controversial issues. 129 footnotes.

92. Daugherty, D. A. (1988). *Separation of Powers and Abuses in Prosecutorial Discretion.* **Journal of Criminal Law and Criminology**, 79 (3), 953-996.

This article discusses the recent Supreme Court decision of *Morrison v. Olson*, which upheld the constitutionality of the independent counsel provision of the Ethics in Government Act. In *Morrison* the Court held that Articles II and III of the U.S. Constitution were not violated by the appointment and removal procedures of the independent counsel provision. Further, the Court held that the independent counsel scheme did not violate the Constitution's separation of governmental powers doctrine. The article, on the other hand, argues that the independent counsel provisions of the Ethics in Government Act provide insufficient safeguards to ensure that independent counsel are accountable and that they not abuse their prosecutorial discretion. 317 footnotes.

93. Davis, M., & Elliston, F. (1986). **Ethics and the Legal Profession**. Buffalo, NY: Prometheus.

This edited volume covers the legal profession, moral critiques of professionalism, the adversary system, conflicts of interest, perjury, confidentiality, and the provision of legal services. An introductory historical section provides information on the development of moral standards in the legal profession, and analyzes the lawyer's role within the contemporary criminal justice system.

94. Douglass, J. J. (1988). **Ethical Issues in Prosecution**. Houston, TX: College of District Attorneys, 560 p.

Relevant case law and standards relating to prosecutorial responsibilities during the pretrial phase are reviewed, including those relating to investigation and discovery, charging, and plea negotiations. Discussion focuses on prosecutorial relations with jurors, decorum in the courtroom, forensic irresponsibility, argument, and media relations. Emphasis is on providing prosecutors with guidance in developing a sense of professional responsibility in their management of whatever situations may arise in a case. Standards developed by the American Bar Association and the National District Attorneys' Association are discussed. Chapter footnotes, table of cases cited, and a 45-item bibliography are provided.

95. Elliston, F. A., & Van Schaick, J. (1984). **Legal Ethics: An Annotated Bibliography and Resource Guide**. Littleton, CO: Fred B. Rothman & Co., 190 p.

This is an annotated bibliography focusing on ethical writings of relevance to the legal profession. Chapters describe professional codes and rules, legal education, the lawyer's role, the practice of law as a business, the courts, and the philosophy of law. Additional topics covered include professional conflicts of interests, advertising, prosecutorial discretion, plea bargaining, confidentiality, perjury, special interest groups, and law school textbooks.

96. *Ethics of Expert Testimony.* (1986). **Law and Human Behavior,** 10 (1-2), 177 p. NOTE: Entire Volume.

These thirteen papers and an introduction present the perspectives of psychologists, legal scholars, and ethicists on the ethics of expert testimony by experimental psychologists. The papers are the product of a 1983 conference held at Johns Hopkins University. The articles clarify the major ethical questions facing the prospective expert witness, including whether the expert's role is advocate or educator, possible unanticipated effects of the expert's testimony on jurors, and what constitutes an adequate basis for a statement by an expert witness. Alternative positions on these issues are defined and debated. The papers also discuss the fundamentals of moral reasoning and make clear the realities of interaction with a judicial system that subjects the psychologist to a variety of pressures and limitations. Figures, tables, footnotes, and chapter reference lists are provided.

97. Feldman, S. W. (1985). *Ethics Workshop: Prosecutorial Interference With Defense Access to Prospective Witnesses.* **Criminal Law Bulletin,** 21 (4), 353-367.

This paper discusses the substantive and procedural aspects of a defendant's right of pretrial access to prospective prosecution witnesses. Constitutional rights are reviewed, including those pertaining to due process, the right to counsel, and the guarantee of compulsory process. Relevant court decisions applying these rights to defense access to witnesses are analyzed. American Bar Association Standards on the Prosecution and Defense Function are cited, as well as the ABA's Model Code of Professional Responsibility, to highlight ethical considerations which support defense pretrial access to witnesses. The paper suggests steps defense counsel may take in attempting to obtain pretrial access to an apparently reluctant witness. A total of 107 footnotes are provided.

98. Freedman, M. H. (1984). *Lawyer-Client Confidences Under the ABA Model Rules: Ethical Rules Without Ethical Reason.* **Criminal**

Justice Ethics, 3 (2), 3-8.

This article examines the American Bar Association ethical guidelines for exceptions to lawyer-client relationships, proposes considerations to be used in weighting these exceptions, and provides a proposed reordering of exceptions. Under the ABA model rules, disclosure is required to rectify a fraud perpetrated on the court or to obey court orders. It is forbidden when it serves to prevent substantial financial loss to third parties caused by the client's wrongful conduct. It is suggested that this ranking is a grotesque caricature of an ethical standard and is indefensible via any rational ethical analysis. It is further suggested that exceptions to confidentiality be ranked by taking into account the purpose for the confidentiality rule, by making a judgment regarding the intrinsic value of each exception, by considering the availability of other means for achieving the same ends as an exception, and by avoiding fallacious arguments. Included are 7 footnotes.

99. Fretz, D. R. (1975). **Ethics for Judges,** 2ed. Reno, NV: National College of the State Judiciary, 48 p.

Intended as a textbook for judges, this volume describes the nature of ethics and attempts to explain why ethics are important for judges. The ABA Code of Judicial Conduct is presented and discussed, potential problem areas are identified, and information is presented on how to obtain advice on ethical questions. A concluding chapter outlines possible sanctions for judicial misconduct. An appendix describing the composition and jurisdiction of the ABA Standing Committee on Ethics and Professional Responsibility is provided.

100. Goldberg, M. S. (1983). *Publication Rights Agreements in Sensational Criminal Cases: A Response to the Problem.* **Cornell Law Review,** 68 (5), 686-705.

This article suggests that statutes are required to deal with problems created by massive public interest in sensational crimes. These problems include: (1) the risk of inadequate representation, (2) unjust enrichment of guilty defendants, (3) insufficient compensation to crime victims, and (4) the endangerment of defendants' constitutional rights. Providing a contingency for defense attorneys' fees when significant funds are available from the publication of the defendant's story would allow defendants to use their publication proceeds only for defense until a verdict is reached. Attorneys' fees would be negotiated, and most of the publication proceeds would be held in escrow for the victims. In cases of conviction, the victims would receive all money remaining in escrow accounts after attorneys collect their fees. Acquitted defendants would receive all remaining escrow money. Contingent attorneys' fees would ensure attorneys optimum financial gains, reduce defendant claims of ineffective counsel, and preserve defendants' First Amendment rights. These fee arrangements would also eliminate the appearance of impropriety, reduce the state's defense cost, and help relieve overcrowded court dockets. Ninety footnotes are provided.

101. Goldman, A. H. (1984). *Confidentiality, Rules, and Codes of Ethics.* **Criminal Justice Ethics**, 3 (2), 8-14.

Following a discussion of M. H. Freedman's (1984) analysis and weighting of conditions which might justify exceptions to the confidentiality of lawyer-client communications, difficulties with ethical codes in general and those proposed by the American Bar Association and Freedman in particular are identified. An alternate approach to professional ethics is suggested. Freedman and the ABA are criticized because both assume that the way to guide legal practitioners in moral matters is to devise and teach an enforceable code of ethics. As a substitute for such codes, the article suggests, reasonable training in ethics should be required. Lawyers should acquire extensive experience in reasoning and arguing about complex moral cases and learn to identify and weigh reasons in favor of a course of action. The article suggests that lawyers trained in this way, if morally well intentioned, could be better trusted to act ethically than could those bound by the rules of a code

102. Green, B. A. (1988). *The Ethical Prosecutor and the Adversary System.* **Criminal Law Bulletin**, 24 (2), 126-145.

The author of this article, a former federal prosecutor and clerk with the U.S. Supreme Court, takes issue with virtually every point made in an earlier issue of the Criminal Law Bulletin, which dealt with subtle problems of prosecutorial misconduct. An interesting analysis is provided of the boundary between behavior that is permitted by the system and behavior that could truly be considered misconduct.

103. Gregg, R. (1989). *Legal and Ethical Considerations.* In Everstine, Diane & Everstine, Louis, **Sexual Trauma in Children and Adolescents: Dynamics and Treatment.** New York, NY: Brunner/Mazel, 174-196.

Ethical and legal factors to consider in assessing and treating the sexual abuse of children and adolescents are explored. Such factors figure prominently in clinician recordkeeping, court procedures, the criminal process, suspect identification, and the district attorney's role in filing criminal actions. The rationale for, and process of, criminal and civil proceedings are described. From ethical and legal arguments, the author concludes that legal judgments convey a message that society recognizes the unacceptability of sexual trauma to children and adolescents. 10 references are provided.

104. Hobbs, S. (1988). *Judicial Discipline and Due Process in Washington State: In re Deming.* **Washington Law Review,** 63 (3), 725-748.

This article analyzes due process rights in judicial disciplinary proceedings, and focuses on the conflict between the need to discipline judges who violate ethical or behavioral standards and the need to protect judicial autonomy. *In re Deming,* a judicial disciplinary case decided by the supreme court of the state of Washington, raised three due process issues concerning: (1) the elements that constitute adequate notice and an opportunity to be heard, (2) the concentration of investigatory, prosecutory, and adjudicatory powers in one institution violating the appearance of fairness doctrine, and (3) the due process rights of a judge accused of misconduct. The court identified eleven procedural protections to which every judge charged of misconduct is entitled. 122 footnotes are provided.

105. Ingraham, B. L. (1987). *Ethics of Testimony: Conflicting Views on the Role of the Criminologist as Expert Witness.* In Anderson, Patrick L., et al. (eds.), **Expert Witnesses.** Albany, NY: State University of New York Press, 178-199.

The author suggests that criminologists are not ethically justified in testifying as experts in judicial proceedings because the process cannot, by reason of its structure and the people who operate it, lead to an objective understanding of scientific knowledge. The expert witness is manipulated by the system in such a way that it is possible to develop two or more conflicting expert witnesses. For this reason, the expert witness testimony of professionals within the field of psychiatry, in particular, has lost its legal credibility. Eleven footnotes are given.

106. Jonakait, R. N. (1987). *Ethical Prosecutor's Misconduct.* **Criminal Law Bulletin,** 23 (6), 550-567.

This article maintains that the primary causes of prosecutorial misconduct are endemic to the criminal justice system, and that only systemic reform can preserve the integrity of the trial process. According to the author the justice system does not see prosecutorial misconduct as an important problem, viewing prosecutors as at least as fair, honorable, and honest as other attorneys. The claim is made that aberrant pressures are not the major cause of prosecutorial misconduct. Instead, the forces that impel it are seen to exist in routine cases for ordinary prosecutors.

107. Kittel, N. G. (1987). *Criminal Defense Attorneys: Bottom of the Legal Profession's Class System?* **The Justice Professional,** 2 (1), 44-59.

A substantial literature portrays criminal defense attorneys as enjoying poor ethics, sordid working conditions, or low public and professional esteem. Despite this literature, a very substantial majority of the attorneys surveyed in this study did not desire to change careers. This response and the comments made by study group members do not indicate a demoralized sample, but show a group evidencing considerable satisfaction with their professional careers. This satisfaction runs across the entire range of the professional group without regard to the number of years an individual practiced law or his or her status as a private practitioner or public defender.

108. Kleinig, J. (1989). *The Selling of Jury Deliberations.* **Criminal Justice Ethics,** 8 (1), 26.

This brief article is an editor's introduction to three invited commentaries on issues raised in the wake of the famous Howard Beach trial. While jury deliberations were in process an attempt was made to sell information from the jury's deliberations to the press. Following the trial, at least one newspaper made independent efforts to buy a juror's journal of the deliberations. The author suggests that the freedom of the press may be adversely affected if it is prohibited from offering financial incentives to secure information.

109. Kunan, J. S. (1983). **How Can You Defend these People?** New York, NY: Random House.

This volume includes a series of essays which focus upon the demands of defending apparently guilty clients. The responsibilities of defense attorneys are outlined, and a case made for defending guilty clients. The American Bar Association's *Code of Professional Responsibility* is discussed, and the need for high standards internal to the legal profession is stressed. Chapter footnotes.

110. Letman, S. T., Edwards, D. W., & Bell, D. J. (1984). **Legal Issues in Criminal Justice: The Courts.** Cincinnati, OH: Pilgrimage, 256 p.

This is a series of papers dealing with court issues such as the closure of judicial proceedings, federal habeas corpus doctrine, pretrial diversion, the insanity defense, plea bargaining, capital punishment, law and ethics, and trends in court reform. An analysis of constitutional issues in pretrial diversion processing identifies rationales for such activity. Aspects of the insanity defense, including the criteria for the four basic insanity defenses, are also considered. An included essay on law and ethics discusses the professional role and responsibilities of lawyers. Chapter notes are provided.

111. Luban, D. (1988). **Lawyers and Justice: An Ethical Study.** Princeton, NJ: Princeton University Press, 440 p.

This book challenges the legal profession's established ethical perspectives, with special focus on the adversarial system. The author charges that the trial process, and the bar in particular, do not seek justice -- only single-minded representation of the client's interests. Public-interest law firms are cited as exemplary representatives of positive moral activity in a social context. An index, bibliography, and table of cases are provided.

112. Lubet, S. (1984). **Beyond Reproach: Ethical Restrictions on the Extrajudicial Activities of State and Federal Judges.** Chicago, IL: American Judicature Society, 66 p.

This monograph describes the sections of the Code of

Judicial Conduct that relate to off-the-bench judicial behavior, and discusses the purposes of regulating such conduct. It also examines case law pertaining to the code regarding the business and financial activities of judges, their civil and charitable activities, and their social activities. It concludes with an assessment of the code's effectiveness and with suggestions for its future development. A table of cases and footnotes are supplied.

113. McCloskey, M., Egeth, H., & McKenna, J. (1986). *The Experimental Psychologist in Court.* **Law and Human Behavior**, 1 (1-2), 1-13.

This introduction to a collection of thirteen papers examines the perspectives of psychologists, legal scholars, and philosophers on the ethics of expert testimony by experimental psychologists. The papers were originally presented at a 1983 conference held at Johns Hopkins University. The articles themselves focus on the major ethical questions facing the prospective expert witness, including whether the expert's role is advocate or educator, the possible unanticipated effects of the expert's testimony on jurors, and what constitutes an adequate basis for a statement by an expert witness. Alternative positions on these issues are defined and debated. The papers also discuss the fundamentals of moral reasoning and make clear the realities of interaction with a judicial system that subjects the psychologist to a variety of pressures and limitations. Many footnotes and 33 references are provided.

114. McDonald, W. F., Cramer, J. A., & Rossman, H. H. (1980). *Prosecutorial Bluffing and the Case Against Plea Bargaining.* In McDonald, W. F. and Cramer, J. A. **Plea-Bargaining, 1980.** Lexington, MA: Lexington Books, 23 p.

Prosecutorial bluffing is examined with regard to its meaning and frequency, the extent to which it is accompanied by elaborate frauds, and the degree to which it involves illegal or unethical behavior. The article describes a national study of plea-bargaining in which bluffing was one of many issues evaluated via the use of open-ended, unstructured interviews with prosecutors. Interviews demonstrated that bluffing does not typically involve violations of legal or ethical norms, elaborate frauds to sustain deceptions, or cases in which no chance existed that the defendant would be convicted at trial. Prosecutors were found to be restrained in their bluffing not only by law and codes of ethics, but also by unofficial norms of the work place. References and tables showing interview responses are included.

115. Maeder, T. (1985). **Crime and Madness - The Origins and Evolution of the Insanity Defense**. New York, NY: Harper and Row Publishers, 219 p.

This book presents an historical, theoretical, and ethical analysis of the insanity defense. The history of the insanity defense is traced from its origins in Christian ethics and Roman jurisprudence, through British laws requiring guilty intent, to the McNaughton rule and subsequent case law developments. The confluence of a number of factors in the 1960's and 1970's, including attention to patient's rights and changes in statutes regarding commitment of the mentally ill, contributed to moves to reform the insanity defense. Many States opted for a guilty-but-mentally-ill verdict. Others called for abolition of the insanity defense. However, the question of responsibility lies at the very heart of the criminal justice system. It is concluded that the insanity defense should be retained because it permits forgiveness where there is no blame, although the defendant in such cases should not be naively absolved of all responsibility. While the defendant may be relieved of criminal responsibility and legal guilt, there is a moral and practical duty that society's compassion is not rewarded by further harm. Source notes and an index are provided.

116. Mann, K. (1985). **Defending White Collar Crime: A Portrait of Attorneys at Work**. New Haven, CT: Yale University Press, 280 p.

This book is based upon research conducted on the New York City white collar criminal defense bar (mostly ex-government lawyers now working the financial districts of Wall Street or Grand Central Station), and on the author's personal experience as a lawyer for a white collar defense firm. The author suggests that while the street-criminal's lawyer focuses on plea bargaining, the white collar criminal's lawyer routinely attempts to have a case discharged at the investigative or pre-indictment stage. The fundamental problem of the white collar attorney is deciding when and how to cooperate with the government. The book devotes three chapters to sources of information, and three more to information control.

117. Martin, B. S. (1984). *Incriminating Criminal Evidence: Practical Solutions*. **Pacific Law Journal**, 15 (3), 807-877.

This article discusses aspects of attorney-client privilege law pertaining to implicating evidence and analyzes the evidentiary, constitutional, criminal, and ethical laws applicable to implicating evidence situations in California. The constitutional ramifications of an attorney's handling of implicating evidence is discussed, focusing on a defendant's right to effective assistance of counsel, the defendant's right against self-incrimination, and the protection that the attorney-client privilege affords these rights. Action taken by attorneys in dealing with implicating evidence is analyzed to determine whether the attorney's conduct constitutes ineffective assistance of counsel or malpractice under present law. The article also focuses on crimes that an attorney may commit when dealing with implicating evidence, emphasizing the crime of destruction or concealment of evidence. The article makes specific recommendations for advice to clients and third parties who inform attorneys about implicating evidence or who bring the evidence to an attorney's office. Specific U.S. Supreme Court decisions are examined. A total of 287 case notes are supplied.

118. ___. (1987). *The Garrow Case Revisited: A Lesson for the Serial Murderer's Counsel.* **Criminal Justice Journal**, 9 (2), 197-239.

This article reviews serial murder cases in general and the 1973 *Garrow* case, in particular. It describes the ethical duty of confidentiality held by the serial murderer's attorney. The article concludes that, according to case law, a New York defense counsel for an obviously insane serial murderer could disclose information to a victim's parents under certain circumstances. Also discussed are exceptions to the duty of confidentiality when an attorney is required by law to divulge information or when an attorney is accused of criminal or professional misconduct growing out of representation of the client. The article suggests that the inevitable discovery exception to the exclusionary rule should apply if any clues leading to the client are discovered as a result of disclosure. 205 footnotes are provided.

119. Martyn, S. R. (1981). *Lawyer Competence and Lawyer Discipline: Beyond the Bar?* **Georgetown Law Journal**, 69 (3), 705-743.

This article examines the role of the bar disciplinary process as a means of ensuring lawyer competence, the bar grievance process, alternative competency controls, and the future role of the bar. Today, over two-thirds of the states have integrated the bar by requiring membership of all attorneys. It is suggested that the traditional grievance process is ineffective because of the lack of resources and the self-protective attitude of the bar. Existing alternative competency controls, such as bar entry standards, process measures (peer review), performance measures, and public control through legislation are all said to be deficient in some respect and cannot serve as adequate enforcement mechanisms. Recommended reforms that would ensure satisfactory discipline and competency are said to include increased publicity in the grievance process; increased lay representation at the screening, investigation and hearing stages; and a requirement that grievance administrators monitor civil malpractice suits. The article provides 292 footnotes.

120. Morse, S. J. (1985). *Excusing the Crazy: The Insanity Defense Reconsidered.* **Southern California Law Review,** 58 (3), 777-836.

Following an examination of the insanity defense, criticisms of and alternatives to the defense are presented, as are the grounds for its utility. Basic moral issues in the insanity defense, such as whether it is just to hold responsible and punish a person who was exceedingly irrational at the time of offense, are examined. The defense is seen as rooted in moral principles of excuse that are accepted in both ordinary human interaction and in criminal law, i.e., that there is no just punishment without desert, and no desert without responsibility. Arguments against the defense are said to confuse causation with excuse, or moral and legal concepts with medical concepts. Other arguments against the defense, such as that it produces wrong verdicts or that assessment of past mental state is too difficult, are also considered. It is concluded that the insanity defense is morally necessary and that substantive and procedural reforms can yield a limited and just insanity defense. A total of 168 footnotes are provided.

121. National American Indian Court Judges Association. (1981). **Model Code of Judicial Conduct for Indian Court Judges.** Washington, D.C.: U.S. Department of the Interior, Bureau of Indian Affairs, 19 p.

This is a model code of judicial conduct for American Indian court judges. The overall purpose of the code is to encourage a spirit of fairness toward persons brought before Indian courts and to ensure fundamental equity and due process in Indian court proceedings. The code is meant to apply to anyone, whether or not a lawyer, who is an officer of a tribal judicial system and who is performing judicial functions. The general requirements of the code hold that Indian judges should: maintain the integrity and independence of the Indian judiciary; avoid impropriety and the appearance of impropriety in all their activities; perform the duties of the office impartially and diligently, and; engage in activities to improve the law, the legal system, and the administration of justice. The code also suggests that Indian judges should regulate their extra-judicial activities to minimize the risk of conflict with judicial duties, and indicates that they should refrain from political activity inappropriate to their judicial office. Aspects of the implementation of each of these standards are discussed. It is expected that tribes will modify some provisions of the code to reflect tribal customs.

122. Ozar, D. T., Kelly, C., & Begue, Y. (1988). *Ethical Conduct of State Court Employees and Administrators: The Search for Standards.* **Judicature**, 71 (5), 262-276.

This article discusses the need for ethical standards of conduct for state court employees and administrators. Two questions in particular are addressed: (1) what ethical standard governs how the duties of court employees are carried out, and (2) who supervises the employees to ensure that their behavior is ethical? The article is based upon a survey of state court administrators. Three states (Arizona, Maryland, and Wisconsin) reported they had ethics codes that applied to court employees. The authors also studied state employee codes as well as statutory and personnel policies. They found that provisions governing confidentiality and political activity among state court employees vary widely. The authors conclude that most states need detailed and systematic codes of ethical conduct for state court employees and administrators. 2 tables, 1 figure, and 56 footnotes are provided.

123. Pellicciotti, J. M. (1987). *Ethics and Criminal Defense: A Client's Desire to Testify Untruthfully.* **The Justice Professional**, 2 (2), 78-91.

The overriding function of the criminal justice profession is to attempt to do justice. The criminal defense attorney advances that function through zealous and loyal representation of the client. Ethical demands require such representation, as well as moral firmness and good faith conduct by the defense attorney. When these demands conflict, ethical balances must be struck. A particular form of balance is required when the defense attorney's client desires to testify untruthfully. This article considers the propriety of remedial measures undertaken by the attorney to deal with client perjury. For known perjury, it advocates an active response of rectification by disclosure.

124. Redlich, N. (1984). **Standards of Professional Conduct for Lawyers and Judges**. Boston, MA: Little Brown, 320 p.

> This text reproduces model codes, standards, and statutes setting forth guidelines for the professional conduct of lawyers and judges. The first section, for lawyers, contains the American Bar Association's (ABA) model code for professional responsibility, ABA model rules for professional conduct, and ABA standards for criminal justice as they relate to prosecutorial and defense functions. The second section, for judges, contains the ABA code of judicial conduct and ABA standards for criminal justice dealing with the special functions of the trial judge. Also included are statutory provisions regarding retirement for disability, procedures for discipline of federal judges, and bias and disqualification of federal judges. The California Code of Judicial Conduct is also included.

125. Roche, J. L. (1987). *Juvenile Court Dispositional Alternatives: Imposing a Defense Duty.* **Santa Clara Law Review,** 27 (2), 279-297.

> This article advocates the adoption of a legally enforceable ethical duty, on the part of the attorney defending a juvenile, to present dispositional alternatives to the juvenile court. According to present practice, the defense attorney often offers no alternatives because he or she is ill-prepared to do so; or because counsel perceives defense responsibilities to be limited to only advising the client to admit or deny allegations, or as confined to arguing the legal merits of relevant defenses. It is suggested that the defense attorney has an ethical duty to propose alternatives that are in the best interests of the minor client, and that to do less results in inadequate representation of the client. The author suggests that this ethical duty ought to be imposed by a rule of court requiring all counsel defending juveniles to

file a dispositional plan with the court. 99 footnotes are
included.

126. Rosen, R. A. (1988). *Disciplinary Sanctions Against Prosecutors
for Brady Violations: A Paper Tiger.* **Criminal Law Review,** 459-508.
NOTE: Reprinted from 65 N.C.L. Rev. 693 (1987).

A survey of the relevant literature and of lawyer disciplinary bodies in all 50 states and the District of
Columbia was conducted to examine rules that impose a
duty on prosecutors to reveal exculpatory evidence, and
which prohibit the presentation of false evidence, while
providing sanctions for violations of such rules. Taken
together with constitutional standards, these disciplinary
codes provide a comprehensive network of prohibitions
that outlaw prosecutorial misconduct. According to the
author, however, while the disciplinary system appears
to be a deterrent to prosecutorial misconduct, its impact
has been weakened by lax enforcement. Thus, prosecutors have little incentive to refrain from misbehavior.
To correct this problem, it is suggested that bar disciplinary bodies should review reported cases of misconduct
and initiate disciplinary proceedings, and that courts
should adopt a bad-faith standard and forcefully reverse
convictions on suppressed exculpatory or false evidence.
278 footnotes are included.

127. Scott, C. F. (1988). *Reconciling Conflicts in Illinois Judicial
Ethics.* **Loyola University of Chicago Law Journal,** 19 (3), 1067-
1095.

The Illinois Code of Judicial Conduct is examined in
order to identify the limits on, and allowable latitude
for, a judge's conduct on incidental ethical questions,
and to specify how the new code affects a judge's judicial, civic, personal, charitable, and political roles. The
article specifies permissible judicial conduct in a judge's
relationship with attorneys, a judge's responsibility
regarding the accepting of gifts, bequests, favors or
loans from lawyers who practice or have practiced
before him or her, and caveats on *ex parte* communications. The article also details when a judge must disqualify him or herself from future consideration of a
case. Also discussed are the judge's right to withdraw
from a case, appropriate judicial conduct while on the
bench, the impact of judges' sexual transgressions,
appropriate judicial behavior regarding political activities and campaigns, and the appropriate judicial response on learning that a fellow judge has violated a

rule of judicial conduct. 151 footnotes are included.

128. Sharrow, R. M. (1986). *Should Lawyers Advertise?* **Maryland Bar Journal**, April 1986, 14-17.

Since the landmark Supreme Court case of *Bates v. State Bar of Arizona* lawyer advertising has been permitted. This article debates the pros and cons of lawyer advertising and concludes that advertising positively impacts the legal profession. The author suggests that public opinion about the practice of law has improved since advertising began, and argues that advertising is a tool for the education of the public.

129. Shea, E. F. (1986). *Should Lawyers Advertise?* **Maryland Bar Journal**, April 1986, 14-15, 17.

In answer to Sharrow (above) this article argues that lawyer advertising has negatively impacted the public perception of lawyers. The legal profession is seen as one which should place ethics and values above the drive for monetary gain. Shoddy and bargain basement advertisement is seen as particularly harmful to the values inherent in the practice of law.

130. Shonholtz, R. (1984). *Neighborhood Justice Systems: Work, Structure, and Guiding Principles.* **Mediation Quarterly**, (5), 3-30.

The nation's first neighborhood-based justice system (the Boards Program) is discussed. The goals, values, and ethics involved in developing neighborhood self-governance and dispute resolution are reviewed. Some of the myths surrounding programs of this type are exposed. The author suggests that this kind of democratic activity depends upon the community's capacity to manage internal conflicts, support its own conflict resolution services, and train its residents. One figure is included.

131. Spaeth, E. B. (1988). *Limitations on the Effectiveness of Criminal Defense Counsel: Legitimate Means of "Chilling Wedges?" (A Symposium).* **University of Pennsylvania Law Review**, 136 (6), 1779-1973.

Eight papers examine ethical dilemmas and limitations on the effectiveness of defense counsel. The issue of when the government can subpoena defense counsel to testify before a grand jury is considered. Problems posed by rules of professional conduct that discourage or prohibit an attorney in a case from being a witness in that case and the effect of a subpoena on the attorney-client relationship and communications are discussed. Issues raised by investigations of criminal defense counsel suspected of criminal wrongdoing are examined, particularly with respect to the use of investigative techniques such as electronic surveillance that may intrude into the zone of legitimate client-attorney relations. Finally, the effects of various limitations on defense counsel that affect the client's Sixth Amendment rights are examined, as are the scope of those rights, the effects of forfeiture provisions that require counsel to forfeit fees that came from the proceeds of a criminal enterprise, and other intrusions and limitations on the attorney-client relationship.

132. Stern, M. D. & Hoffman, D. (1988). *Privileged Informers: The Attorney Subpoena Problem and a Proposal for Reform.* **University of Pennsylvania Law Review,** 136 (6), 1783-1854.

This paper examines the government's use of subpoenas requiring defense attorneys to testify before a grand jury, associated ethical dilemmas, and possible solutions. The author claims that the cited practice represents a sharp break with the traditions and expectations on which the American legal system is based and has resulted in the disruption or destruction of the attorney-client relationship. Because of significant gaps in the coverage of existing attorney-client and work-product privileges, some discoverable information in an attorney's possession can usually be obtained by a prosecutor determined to make the attorney a witness. Faced with the unwelcome prospect of compelling attorneys to testify against their own clients, some courts have attempted to close gaps in the area of privilege, while others have used their supervisory powers to regulate the use of attorney subpoenas. New safeguards have failed to keep pace with the government's changing investigative and prosecutorial strategies. Four reforms are proposed to restore the balance between the individual's right to counsel and the government's need for evidence. Guidelines and resolutions on the use of attorney subpoenas are appended. 305 footnotes are supplied.

133. Subin, H. I. (1988). *A Criminal Lawyer's "Different Mission:" Reflections on the "Right" to Present a False Case.* **Criminal Law Review,** 511-539. NOTE: Reprinted from **Georgetown Journal of Legal Ethics** 125 (1987).

This article explores the lawyer's roles as client representative and officer of the court, and attempts to define
the limits on the methods a lawyer should be willing to
use when the client's goals are inconsistent with the
truth.   Focus is on the use of three legal techniques for
subverting the truth: (1) the cross-examination of a
truthful government witness in order to undermine his
or her testimony or credibility, (2) direct presentation of
testimony to discredit truthful evidence or accredit a
false theory, and (3) arguments to the jury based on any
of these acts. The author holds that although the prosecution has the burden of proving guilt and the defense
attorney has the right and obligation to challenge the
government's proof to ensure its accuracy and to remain
passive in the presentation of facts to the jury, the
defense attorney does not have a duty or right to subvert the truth.   A new rule of conduct is proposed that
holds it improper for an attorney who knows beyond a
reasonable doubt the truth of a fact established in the
state's case, to attempt to refute that fact through
argument or the introduction or impeachment of evidence. 119 footnotes are provided.

134. United Nations. (1985). **Formulation and Application of
United Nations Standards and Norms in Criminal Justice: Guide-
lines on the Independence of the Judiciary.** New York, NY:
United Nations, 14 p.

Guidelines on the independence of the judiciary
emphasize that justice requires that everyone be entitled to a fair and public hearing by a competent, independent, and impartial tribunal. The guidelines deal
with the concepts of independence and impartiality and
the principle of separation of judicial functions from
other functions of the government. The guidelines also
stipulate that judges have freedom of expression and
association. Provisions discuss judicial qualifications,
selection, and pre-service and in-service training;
promotion and transfer; and tenure. Other provisions
discuss professional duties and immunity, and deal with
such issues as confidentiality, disqualification, discipline,
and removal. The role of the judiciary in court management is also considered. 2 notes are included.

135. Uviller, R. H. (1990). *The Embarrassment of Rudolph Giuliani.*
Criminal Justice Ethics, 9 (1), 3-10.

This article describes the situation of ethical lawyers

who appear to be tainted in the public view by their association with unethical clients. It focuses on the question of whether lawyers who have represented unsavory clients should fairly expect to have reputations assailed if they seek public office. The extent to which a candidate's professional history is relevant to a consideration of qualifications for public office is discussed. It is concluded that the ethical distance inherent in professional relationships will not satisfy all inquiries into the character of individual lawyers.

136. Volcansek, M. L. (1980). *Codes of Judicial Ethics: Do They Affect Judges' Views of Proper Off-The-Bench Behavior?* **American Business Law Journal**, 17 (Winter), 493-505.

To determine the extent to which more stringent cannons of ethics would influence judicial perceptions of appropriate judicial conduct, a questionnaire was mailed to the 210 sitting district judges in Texas. Texas district judges were chosen for two reasons: a new stricter code has recently replaced a loose code, and a stratified sampling of 62 of these judges, interviewed in 1973, allowed for a measure of change. Questionnaires covered two types of judicial conduct outside the actual decisional process: (1) public and business involvement and (2) political activities. Findings suggest that modifications in the code did influence perceptions as to what constitutes proper off-the-bench behavior in the political arena. The findings also suggest that post-Watergate morality may have served as a catalyst both for rewriting the code of ethics and for the restrictive evaluation by the judges as to what constitutes appropriate off-the-bench behavior. Tabular data accompany the article.

137. Weithorn, L. A. (1987). *Professional Responsibility in the Dissemination of Psychological Research in Legal Contexts.* In Melton Gary B. (ed.), **Reforming the Law: Impact of Child Development Research.** New York, NY: Guilford Press, 253-279.

Critical ethical issues and dilemmas raised by the participation of social scientists in legal policy making through their collection and dissemination of research data are discussed. The distortion of truths via the suppression of unconforming data is a concern to behavioral scientists. One of the most important aspects of ethical conduct requires that researchers carefully analyze and balance the compelling ethical concerns associated with the dissemination of legal policy-relevant data. Twenty-five references are provided.

138. Wishman, S. (1981). **Confessions of a Criminal Lawyer.** New York, NY: Random House.

This book provides anecdotes from the life of a criminal lawyer. The author questions his role in defending guilty clients, and describes in detail his part in wrangling a minor sentence for a heinous offender. The book questions the worth of a system that can do apparent injustices in the name of justice.

139. Wright, T. P. (1988). *Prosecutorial Ethics and Values in Plea Bargaining.* **Prosecutor,** 21 (3), 23-28.

The author analyzes the prosecutor's role in plea bargaining, explores the values and ethics deemed most desirable in a prosecutor, and presents a taxonomy for effective plea bargaining. The criminal justice system is described as a pyramid with three principles: (1) liberty and due process, (2) order and public safety, and (3) governmental efficiency and economy. Using this framework, the paper discusses the American Bar Association's *Model Rules for Professional Conduct* and the *Special Responsibilities of a Prosecutor.* A survey of perspectives on prosecutorial ethics concludes that defense of public liberty, while honoring the basic constitutional rights of defendants, seems a moderate and reasonable set of values in approaching crime control. Justifications for plea bargaining, most of which fall within the governmental efficiency and economy principle, are detailed. 22 footnotes are included.

4
Corrections

140. Able, C. F., & Marsh, F. H. (1984). **Punishment and Restitu-
tion: A Restitutionary Approach to Crime and the Criminal.**
Westport, CT: Greenwood Press, 214 p. NOTE: Contributions in
Criminology and Penology Series, No. 5

The author provides an analysis of practical and ethical
issues in current retributive, rehabilitative, and deterrent approaches to crime within the criminal justice
system. The model of retribution is identified as the
fairest, most efficient and workable system. This model
balances the responsibility for the handling of criminals
among the various government agencies, society, victims, and the criminals themselves. Chapter notes, an
index, and approximately 160 references are provided.

141. AIMS Instructional Media. (1987). **The Correctional Officer:
Ethics and Conduct.** Glendale, CA: Aims Instructional Media.
NOTE: VHS video-cassette, color, 20 minutes.

Legal and ethical points of view are examined in this
video tape as they apply to correctional institutions.
On-duty and off-duty employee conduct is discussed.
Specific codes of conduct are defined. The paramilitary
command structure of correctional institutions is
examined. Policies in the areas of: abusive language,
use of force, favoritism, and personal contact with
inmates and their families are discussed.

142. American Correctional Association. (1990). **Standards for Adult Correctional Institutions**, 3ed. Laurel, MD: American Correctional Association, 220 p.

> This is a third revision of the American Correctional Association's (ACA) standards for institutional management. 463 standards cover a wide range of topics, including safety, emergency procedures, security, control, inmate rules, discipline, staff development, the physical plant, medical care, health, floor space, religion, and inmate rights. Institutions meeting ACA standards are eligible for accreditation under the Association's facility certification program. Also available in the form of a 180 page supplement to earlier editions.

143. American Psychological Association. (1980). **Who Is the Client? The Ethics of Psychological Intervention in the Criminal Justice System.** Washington, D.C.: American Psychological Association Publications, 174 p.

> The Task Force on the Role of Psychology in the Criminal Justice System provides its report along with five background papers centering on the main areas where psychologists experience a great deal of ethical confrontation. The papers include: policing, court systems, corrections, juvenile justice programs, and various other subtopics. This detailed report suggests twelve ethical standards that psychology, as a profession, should adopt. Papers include problem analysis and recommendations for solving ethical dilemmas.

144. Arboleda-Florez, J. (1983). *Ethics of Psychiatry in Prison Society.* **Canadian Journal of Criminology**, 25 (1), 47-54.

> According to the author, the most viable professional position for psychiatrists to maintain while serving a prison system is on the outside. All too frequently the prison psychiatrist is forced to align with one of three prison social groups: (1) inmates, (2) guards, or (3) administration. Falling into favor, or simply being perceived as having fallen into favor, with any one of these social groups restricts the psychiatrist's ability to perform his or her job properly. It is recommended that the psychiatrist should be retained as a consultant by the prison medical officer when psychiatric services are deemed necessary.

145. Baudouin, J. L. (1985). **Behavior Alteration and the Criminal Law.** Ottawa, Ontario: Law Reform Commission of Canada, 55 p.

Moral and legal issues surrounding physiological and psychological behavior modification techniques authorized under current Canadian law are examined. Physiological techniques which are discussed include pharmacotherapy, electroconvulsive therapy, electrical stimulation, psychosurgery and castration. Psychological techniques include psychotherapy (individual, group and milieu) and behavioral therapies (positive reinforcement, negative reinforcement and desensitization). Some of the legal areas addressed are: (1) the treatment of inmates, and (2) the rights of the involuntary psychiatric patient.

146. Becker, J. V., & Abel, G. G. (1985). *Methodological and Ethical Issues in Evaluating and Treating Adolescent Sexual Offenders.* In Emeline, M. O., et al. (eds.), **Adolescent Sex Offenders: Issues in Research and Treatment**. Rockville, MD: National Institute of Justice, 109-129.

According to the author, various ethical and methodological issues must be given consideration when implementing and evaluating the study of treatment programs for adolescent sex offenders. Ethical issues include the right to privacy and the right to no treatment without consent. Methodological issues include the defining of proper issues to be studied, as well as a consideration of what might be proper models for assessing deviance. Each area must be given full consideration if appropriately applicable norms for defining deviance in need of treatment are to be established.

147. Bedau, H. A. (1985). *Classification-Based Sentencing: Some Conceptual and Ethical Problems.* In J. Roland Pennock and John W. Chapman (eds.), **Criminal Justice**. New York, NY: Columbia University Press, 89-118. NOTE: Revision of a paper originally prepared at the request of the Panel on Sentencing Research, Committee on Research on Law Enforcement and the Administration of Justice, Commission on Behavioral and Social Sciences and Education, of the National Research Council, and presented at the Panel's conference on July 27-29, 1981.

This essay utilizes various ethical perspectives to evaluate proposals made in 1980 by the Pennsylvania Commission on Sentencing. The Commission recommended an offense and offender classification scheme as a means of implementing determinate sentencing throughout the state. Under the Pennsylvania scheme, punitive sentencing derives from assessments of the offender's proper "deserts," measured in terms of the

harm caused by the offense and the offender's culpabili-
ty. The scheme itself is ethically evaluated according to
the severity ranking given offenses compared to one
another, as well as the punitive options mandated for
each ranking. The author identifies ethical concerns at
the post-classification sentencing phase of a criminal
trial as: (1) the legitimacy of the factors introduced to
modify guideline standards, (2) whether the degree of
modification in a given case is defensible, and (3)
whether other post-classification factors ought to be
introduced. 38 notes are included.

148. _____. (1987). **Death is Different: Studies in the Morality,
Law and Politics of Capital Punishment.** Boston, MA: Northeast-
ern University Press, 307 p.

This book brings together ten essays and studies published by the author over the previous decade. Each
essay deals with some aspect of the philosophical and
legal issues involved in capital punishment, and with the
movement toward abolition of the death penalty. The
abolitionist movement is described in political terms,
and its supporters are depicted as involved in a self-
proclaimed moral crusade. Landmark cases, including
Gregg v. Georgia, and *Furman v. Georgia,* are discussed.

149. Berlin, F. S., & Krout, E. (1986). *Pedophilia: Diagnostic
Concepts, Treatment, and Ethical Considerations.* In Haden, Dawn
C. (ed.), **Out of Harm's Way: Readings on Child Sexual Abuse, Its
Prevention and Treatment.** Phoenix, AZ: Oryx Press, 155-171.

See Chapter 5, Victim's Rights

150. Bohmer, C. (1983). *Legal and Ethical Issues in Mandatory
Treatment: The Patient's Rights Versus Society's Rights.* In Greer,
Joanne G., et al. (eds.), **Sexual Aggressor: Current Perspectives on
Treatment.** New York, NY: Van Nostrand Reinhold, 3-21.

This paper addresses the mandatory treatment of sex
offenders through such legal issues as the right to
refuse treatment, informed consent and offender rights
under various treatment modalities. Ethical issues are
viewed in terms of a balancing of rights between the
individual, social institutions, and society. Specific
attention is given to ethical situations which arise
between therapists and patients.

151. Brown, B. S., et al. (1981). *Behavior Modification: Perspective on a Current Issue.* In Wienckowski, L. A., et al. (eds.), **Correctional Counseling and Treatment**. Belmont, CA: Duxbury, 279-323.

An analysis of behavior modification procedures with associated legal and ethical issues is presented. Current behavior modification procedures include desensitization and token economies. According to the author, a study of applicable case law reveals that there has been some abuse of inmates treated under behavior modification schemes in correctional facilities. The position is advanced that ethical responsibilities mandate that clients should be made aware of their program, its goals, and any possible dangers that may be involved, and then be offered the option of voluntary participation.

152. **Capital Punishment.** (1985). New York, NY: H. W. Wilson Company, 166 p. NOTE: Reference Shelf, Vol. 57, No. 2.

This volume presents moral and pragmatic arguments for and against the death penalty. The first section reviews judicial and legislative actions concerning capital punishment that have occurred since 1977, and raises the possibility that executions may once again become public. The second section presents moral and religious arguments against capital punishment by psychiatrists, prison staff, humanitarians, interpreters of Christian doctrine, and prisoners. The argument is made that capital punishment is a cruel and unusual punishment, does not deter crime, and may contribute to increased violence. In the third section, proponents of the death penalty argue that murder is so heinous a crime that justice demands a suitably severe punishment, and that the legal execution of felons can serve as an example to others. It is argued that abolitionists use appeal procedures to subvert the criminal justice system and thwart public will. The final section presents examinations of execution by lethal chemical injection. Medical ethical dilemmas also are discussed. 106 references are provided.

153. Clements, C. B. (1987). *Psychologists in Adult Correctional Institutions: Getting Off the Treadmill.* In Morris, E. K., et al. (eds.), **Behavioral Approaches to Crime and Delinquency: A Handbook of Application, Research, and Concepts.** New York, NY: Plenum, 21 p.

The role of correctional psychologists is discussed

within the realm of their professional competence and
ethical sensitivity. The psychologist's role is shown to
include (1) the welfare of the inmate, (2) intake procedures, (3) effective classification, (4) treatment processes, and (5) coordination with prison staff. Prison programs must be planned, developed and evaluated by the
psychologist. It is suggested that, as professionals,
psychologists must stay abreast of all legal implications
and new research developments within their field.

154. Conrad, P., et al. (1980). *Medicine and Crime: The Search for
the Born Criminal and the Medical Control of Criminality.* In
Conrad, Peter, et al. (eds.), **Deviance and Medicalization: From
Badness to Sickness.** Columbus, OH: Merrill, 215-240.

The authors present a serious argument for the use of
biomedics, behavior modification biotechnics, and
associated programs for the purpose of crime control.
The history of biomedics in criminology is outlined.
Present day uses and legal rulings are presented and
ethical dilemmas associated with various theraputic
strategies are discussed. The conclusion anticipates a
growing ethical acceptance of biomedics as other alternatives to crime control fail. There are five suggested
readings.

155. Costello, J. C., et al. (1987). *Legal and Ethical Duties of
Health Care Professionals to Incarcerated Children.* **Journal of
Legal Medicine,** 8 (2), 191-263.

The ethical dilemma of custodial care versus health
care, as seen by health care professionals serving incarcerated juveniles, is identified. The article describes
how the National Commission on Correctional Health
Care (NCCHC) brought the courts and developers of
standards into agreement on certain basic health care
needs of institutionalized juveniles. Present health care
services are described as not meeting established needs
for a variety of reasons. Health care professionals are
exhorted not to hesitate to critically review present
correctional staff practices, procedures and programs.

156. Cox, D. N. (1988). *Caregiver's Dilemma: The Case of Pedo-
philia.* In Freeman, Richard J., et al. (eds.), **Treatment of Sexual
Aggression: Legal and Ethical Issues.** Burnaby, BC: Simon Fraser
University Criminology Research Center, 75-90.

This chapter reviews a 1979 study involving 77 incarcerated pedophiles. The ethical and legal ramifications of

treating this group are studied. Norms and preferences of the group are provided for comparison. Various conditions affecting treatment situations and settings are discussed. An unbiased theraputic attitude and ethical behavior are suggested as essential for effective treatment.

157. Curran, W. J. (1986). *Ethical Perspectives: Formal Codes and Standards.* In Curran, William J., et al. (eds.), **Forensic Psychiatry and Psychology**. Philadelphia, PA: F.A. Davis Company, 18 p.

This analysis focuses on the formal definitions and standards found in official codes of ethical conduct for forensic psychiatrists and forensic psychologists, and on the ethical concepts and clashes between those values as they relate to mental health efforts supporting the legal and correctional systems. The two types of codes discussed are: (1) general codes that cover the basic professional specialties, and which contain provisions relevant to forensic and legal activities, and (2) the more specific codes and standards that deal directly with forensic and legal applications in psychiatry and psychology. Charts and 85 references are provided.

158. Curran, W. J., & Casscells, W. (1980). *Ethics of Medical Participation in Capital Punishment by Intravenous Drug Injection.* **New England Journal of Medicine**, 302 (4), 226-230.

This article examines ethical, legal, and clinical concerns regarding medical participation in capital punishment by intravenous drug injection. Participation in capital punishment programs by medical professionals can involve a variety of roles, from ordering the substance and preparing it for injection, to injecting the substance, or ordering and supervising the injection by other medical personnel, to monitoring the administration and observing the prisoner throughout the continuous injection of the drug, and lastly, to examining the prisoner and pronouncing death. Both internationally recognized principles condemning capital punishment, and the Hippocratic Oath's definition of physicians as healers who would never kill or harm their patients, are cited as mitigating against physician involvement in this form of capital punishment. Over 20 footnotes are provided.

159. Curran, W. J., et al. (1986). *Mental Health and Justice: Ethical Issues of Interdisciplinary Cooperation.* In Curran, William J., et al.

(eds.), **Forensic Psychiatry and Psychology**. Philadelphia, PA: F. A. Davis, 61-73.

According to the author, ethical and value-oriented conflicts confront mental health professionals who work within criminal justice, correctional, military and public school settings. Conflicts arise between their administrative obligations and ethical obligation to their patients. Various court rulings on mental health professional's obligations toward administrators and clients are discussed.

160. _____. (1986). *Ethical Perspectives: Formal Codes and Standards.* In Curran, William J., et al. (eds.), **Forensic Psychiatry and Psychology**. Philadelphia, PA: F.A. Davis, 18 p.

According to the author, codes of conduct are sometimes responsible for conflicting ethical values found in mental health-related issues within legal and correctional settings. The formal definitions and standards found in official codes of ethical conduct for forensic psychiatrists and forensic psychologists are fully discussed. Codes are broken into two main types: general and specific. General codes deal with basic professional specialties while specific codes deal with individual standards relative to the forensic and legal application of psychiatry and psychology. Several charts and 85 references are included.

161. David, M. (1985). *How To Make the Punishment Fit the Crime.* In J. Roland Pennock & John W. Chapman (eds.), **Criminal Justice**. New York, NY: Columbia University Press, 119-155. Note: Republished (slightly revised) from **Ethics**, 93 (4), 726-752.

This essay applies retributive principles to the determination of statutory penalties. Retributivism is seen as any theory of punishment claiming that the only acceptable reason for punishing persons is in response for crime commission. The only acceptable reason for punishing offenders with particular severity is said to be that of making the punishment fit the crime, and the fit between punishment and crime is seen as independent of the consequences of the punishment. Utilitarianism, defined as any theory of punishment that makes the fit between punishment and crime depend upon the consequences of the particular punishment, is contrasted with the retributive perspective. The study concludes that the retributivist penalty is morally superior. 34 notes are provided.

162. **The Death Penalty.** (1986). San Diego, CA: Greenhaven Press, 172 p. NOTE: Opposing viewpoints series.

In addition to providing an historical perspective on attitudes toward the death penalty, this text provides arguments for and against the use of capital punishment, with a focus on its morality and its effectiveness as a deterrent. Chapter One offers essays written between 1700 and 1928 espousing the morality/immorality and effectiveness/ineffectiveness of the death penalty. Chapter Two includes arguments on the morality versus immorality of the death penalty, its effects on society, and religious arguments for and against its use. Chapter Three considers whether the death penalty deters or incites murder, the validity of deterrence as a justification for the death penalty, and the implications of inconclusive evidence for the validity of deterrence theory. The final chapter brings together opposing views on the use of the death penalty in treason cases through analysis of three sensationalized cases: Sacco and Vanzetti in the 1920's, Julius and Ethel Rosenberg in the 1950's, and John Walker in the 1980's. Each chapter includes exercises designed to increase critical thinking skills. An index and 28-item bibliography are included.

163. Diallo, Y. (1987). *International Co-operation, Training and Research: Implementation of International Instruments on Human Rights.* In Hideo, Utsuro (ed.), **Resource Material Series No. 32.** Tokyo, Japan: UNAFEI, 55-68.

International agreements relative to the treatment of prisoners and detainees are discussed. Issues include: the protection of prisoners and detainees, and outlawing torture and other treatments that are considered cruel or degrading. A code of medical ethics and various principles to protect prisoners from arbitrary arrest, exile, and detention are presented in draft form. Issues pertaining to juveniles, racial discrimination, and apartheid are likewise identified. The role of the United Nations in training workers and governments in these standards is also discussed.

164. DiChiara, A., & Galliher, J. F. (1984). *Thirty Years of Deterrence Research: Characteristics, Causes, and Consequences.* **Contemporary Crises,** 8 (3), 243-263.

This study describes the literature on deterrence research, determines in what ways it has been influenced by funding agencies, and explores the consequences of such research -- including its ideological implications and attendant ethical dilemmas. According to the authors, the increasing tendency to store criminal justice data in computers made such research easier. The study found, for example, the "boom year" for articles on deterrence was 1968. In the 1960's and 1970's, the majority of deterrence articles were empirical studies of deterrence, with studies in the 1970's relying heavily on questionnaires for self-report information on law violation and perceptions of punishment. Methodological innovations, rather than new types or sources of data, are cited to help explain the research boom. Eighty-four notes are listed.

165. Dickens, B. M. (1988). *Legal and Ethical Considerations in Enforced Therapy.* In Freeman, Richard J., et al. (eds.), **Treatment of Sexual Aggression: Legal and Ethical Issues.** Burnaby, BC: Simon Fraser University, 23-52.

Ethical issues involved in the receipt of free and informed consent from incarcerated sex offenders for mandatory or experimental treatment programs are discussed. The availability of free and informed consent is often scarce when an inmate's sentence or early release is directly tied to their consent for treatment. The courts have held that imprisonment does not necessarily interfere with an inmate's ability to give free consent to treatment. However, the offered treatment must be considered routine and acceptable as well as reasonably safe and effective.

166. Drewett, D. (1986). *Doing Philosophy and Doing Time.* **Religious Education,** 81 (4), 625-642.

The author, a Presbyterian minister and librarian for the New York State Department of Correctional Services, discusses his experiences teaching a philosophy course to inmates at Otisville Correctional Facility in New York. Inmates' reflections on the philosophy of imprisonment, limitations on teaching created by the prison environment, and recommendations for future instruction are outlined. 12 footnotes are included.

167. Elliston, F. A. (1985). *Deadly Force and Capital Punishment: A Comparative Appraisal.* In Heffernan, William C., et al. (eds.), **Police Ethics: Hard Choices in Law Enforcement.** New York, NY: John Jay Press, 15 p.

See Chapter 2, The Police

168. Fisher, F. M., & Kadane, J. B. (1983). *Empirically Based Sentencing Guidelines and Ethical Considerations.* In Alfred Blumstein, et al. (eds.), **Research on Sentencing: The Search for Reform.** Washington, D.C.: National Academy Press, 184-193.

The authors suggest that empirically based sentencing guidelines rest upon computerized models which may avoid hard ethical decisions and mislead criminal justice practitioners by substituting statistical sophistication for ethical sophistication. If variables are erroneously omitted from equations underlying the guidelines, the estimated effects will be incorrect and the guidelines misleading. This will be especially important if the omitted variables are ethically relevant, and include such measures as race. Models are presented to illustrate approaches to sentencing formulas where race has influenced past decisions. The question becomes whether sentencing formulas can replace ethical decisions. The ethical choices presented in this article challenge the view that guidelines can or should be based on past behavior rather than constructed directly from ethical or societal considerations. Formula and five footnotes are included.

169. Freeman, R. J. (1988). *Current Treatment for Sexual Offenders: A Non-Evaluative Review.* In Freeman, Richard J., et al. (eds.), **Treatment of Sexual Aggression: Legal and Ethical Issues.** Burnaby, BC: Simon Fraser University, 1-22.

A review of approaches to the treatment of sex offenders and associated legal issues are presented. The use of psychosocial, psychophysiological, cognitive, and biomedical therapies are reviewed. The pros and cons of each type of treatment, as well as combined treatments, are discussed.

170. Freeman, R. J., & Verdun-Jones, S. N. (eds.). (1988). **Treatment of Sexual Aggression: Legal and Ethical Issues.** Burnaby, BC: Simon Fraser University Criminology Research Centre Publications, 142 p.

A brief overview of present day treatment methods for sexual abusers is given. The results of a study of the behaviors and attitudes of unincarcerated pedophiles are presented. The issue of free consent among incar-

cerated sex offenders, and possible treatments and experimental programs are presented. Special ethical considerations and challenging professional situations
facing mental health professionals in treating this
population group are discussed.

171. Gabor, T. (1986). **Prediction of Criminal Behaviour: Statistical Approaches**. Toronto, Canada: University of Toronto Press,
125 p.

The author examines the dangers, limitations, and
ethical dilemmas involved in predicting criminality and
recidivism. He addresses the various aspects of prediction including individual factors, environmental factors,
and statistical methods in prediction. The author suggests that there are serious limitations in the contemporary practice of predicting criminal behavior. The
predictive value of every variable or factor used in
prediction has been challenged, and most have been
criticized on ethical grounds. Factors undermining the
accuracy of scientific predictions of criminality are
methodological flaws, the limitations of offense statistics, the subjective or symbolic nature of some variables,
situational variables affecting human behavior, and the
frequent irrelevance of mathematical techniques to the
predictive ability of a given variable set. In spite of the
unreliability of current predictive methods, they are
judged to be preferable to completely subjective, in-
stinctive decision-making regarding the release, sentencing, and classification of offenders. A 270-item bibliography, and author and subject indexes are provided.

172. Goldsmith, H. R. (1988). *The Role of the Juvenile Probation
Officer Regarding the Adolescent Sex Offender and Related Issues.*
Journal of Offender Counseling, Services and Rehabilitation, 12
(2), 115-122.

The ethical role of the juvenile probation officer is
examined relative to adolescent sex offenders. A
hypothetical model is presented in order to illustrate
the need for role consonant treatment models. The
applicability of the proffered model to other offender
populations is presented. Concomitant issues are explored, especially in relation to standardized regimens
which would facilitate appropriate assessment of referrals, aid staff training, and remain efficacious.

173. Gordon, R. M. (1988). *The Need for Treatment and the Right
to Treatment: A Quid Pro Quo in Canadian Corrections?* In Free-

man, Richard J., et al. (eds.), **Treatment of Sexual Aggression: Legal and Ethical Issues**. Burnaby, BC: Simon Fraser University, 53-73.

The American principle of the "quid pro quo" between individual states' rights to incarcerate offenders, and the ethical obligation to offer mental health treatment to offenders, is discussed within the context of the Canadian mental health system. The Canadian system is said to be experiencing tension resulting from differences between the practice of incarcerating offenders because of a need for treatment on the one hand, and the felt need for a right to treatment on the other. A diversity of legal rulings surrounding this issue are identified as they exist within Canadian Provinces.

174. Gordon, R. M., et al. (1983). *Ethics and Ethical Dilemmas in the Treatment of Sex Offenders.* In Verdun-Jones, Simon N., et al. (eds.), **Sexual Aggression and the Law**. Burnaby, BC: Simon Fraser University, 73-96.

The complex role of today's psychologists who are involved in the treatment of sex offenders encompasses a wide variety of ethical issues. Three basic roles for psychologists are identified: (1) researcher, (2) assessor and (3) treater. Basic ethical issues include: the possible deception of patients or others, the problem of maintaining privacy, coercion, and the possibility of physical or psychological injury. The psychologist's positions in today's criminal justice system and in society are discussed.

175. Greenwood, P. W., & Zimring, F. E. (1985). **One More Chance: The Pursuit of Promising Intervention Strategies for Chronic Juvenile Offenders**. Santa Monica, CA: Rand Corporation, 81 p.

This volume examines the correlates of chronic delinquency, legal and ethical constraints on state-imposed interventions, and promising methods of delinquency prevention and rehabilitation. Five groups of factors are identified as predictive of future offending: (1) family factors, such as poor parenting skills and parental pathology or criminality, (2) biological deficits, such as birth defects or learning disability, (3) poor parental attitudes, including a lack of effective supervision, and a lack of affection, (4) past antisocial and acting-out behaviors, and (5) delinquency history. Promising programs for chronic delinquents are described as providing opportunities for success and improved self-esteem, the facilitation of familial bonds, providing timely and accurate feedback on behavior, and reducing or eliminating negative role models and peer influences. 107 references are included.

176. Haas, K. C., & Inciardi, J. A. (1988). **Challenging Capital Punishment: Legal and Social Science Approaches,** 3ed. Newbury Park, CA: Sage, 304 p. NOTE: Sage Criminal Justice Systems Annual, Vol. 24.

This edited volume explores attempts by various courts to use social science research as ammunition to abolish or support capital punishment. "Death qualified juries" are discussed.

177. Harding, T. W. (1987). *AIDS (Acquired Immune Deficiency Syndrome) in Prison.* **Lancet,** Nov. 28, 1260-1263.

This is a report on an early 1987 survey by the Council of Europe of 17 nations in Western Europe to determine how prison medical and administrative staffs were reacting to the AIDS epidemic. The survey produced evidence that some staffs were not following scientifically and ethically sound procedures. Voluntary testing, confidentiality and isolation practices are discussed in this report. Prevention and awareness programs including the use of condoms, needles, good hygiene and nutrition are described.

178. Harris, G. A. A., et al. (1987). **Counseling the Involuntary and Resistant Client.** Laurel, MD: American Correctional Association, 112 p.

As a guide for correctional counselors, this book addresses the legal, ethical and moral issues surrounding involuntary and resistant clients. The author stresses techniques which involve the use of structure, ignore resistance, maximize choices, and emphasize empathy and timing. Dealing with aggressive, antisocial and substance abusing individuals is also addressed.

179. Hawkins, R., & Alpert, G. P. (1989). **American Prison Systems: Punishment and Justice.** Laurel, MD: American Correctional Association, 480 p.

This well researched volume concerns itself with the development of historical forms of punishment. Flogging, hanging, and other forms of punishment are shown to have led to the use of imprisonment for most of today's offenders. The goals of incarceration are explored, and the role of correctional officers is elaborated. The theme of human rights as a yardstick useful in gauging the efficacy of imprisonment permeates the book.

180. Hoekema, D. A. (1986). *Punishment, the Criminal Law, and Christian Social Ethics.* **Criminal Justice Ethics**, 5 (2), 31-54.

Some of the key principles and themes of Christian theology regarding issues in criminal justice are analyzed. Issues of principle and substance are compared with select legal cases and proceedings. Biblical influences over the need for law and the goals of justice are explained. According to the author the fact that there exists tension among Christians demonstrates the need for ongoing reform for all involved in this area of concern.

181. Keating, J. M. (1985). **Seeking Profit in Punishment: The Private Management of Correctional Institutions**. Washington, D.C.: American Federation of State County and Municipal Employees Publications, 59 p.

A serious look is given the economic, legal, and ethical issues that must be properly addressed before the privatization of prison and jail operations can be undertaken. The author suggests that there is little evidence to support the claims that privately owned systems will represent a significant cost savings over government run systems. Ethical issues, such as the appropriateness of states entrusting the punishment of their citizens to profit-oriented private entities, are discussed. 44 footnotes are included.

182. Kilgour, J. L. (1988). *AIDS in Prisons in England and Wales.* In Fleming, A. F., et al. (eds.), **The Global Impact of AIDS**. New York, NY: Alan R. Liss, Inc., 323-327.

This is a study of prisons in England and Wales. According to the author, prison authorities in those countries view imprisonment as a deprivation of personal liberty, but feel obliged to protect the physical and medical welfare of inmates. Inmates are given the same accessibility to medical advice, medication and treatment as is the general populace. Inmates receive the same infectious disease prevention education available to the public. British prison authorities report fewer incidents of HIV infections than are found in prison systems in the United States and mainland Europe.

183. Lozoff, B., & Braswell, M. (1989). **Inner Corrections: Finding Peace and Peace Making.** Laurel, MD: American Correctional Association, 200 p.

This exceptional book is directed primarily towards offenders rather than correctional administrators or criminal justice practitioners. The book details strategies for self improvement, and evolves around a spiritual theme. The authors show how the heart and mind can work together to create a sense of self-control and personal balance and lead to moral decision-making in all future actions.

184. Macklin, R. (1986). *Predicting Dangerousness and the Public Health Response to AIDS (Acquired Immune Deficiency Syndrome).* **Hastings Center Report,** Special Supplement (December), 16-23.

According to the author, society's felt legal, ethical and practical obligations to isolate AIDS infected individuals is often unjustifiable. Certain types of infected people in certain environments require isolation while others do not. This publication suggests that an AIDS infected homosexual inmate should be isolated from other inmates, while a person in society whose practices do not coincide with high risk activities should not be isolated. The confining of individuals should not be based on test results, but on their lifestyles and on the frequency of high risk activities within those lifestyles. More diligence, suggests the author, is needed on the part of public health programs to educate society as to what constitutes high risk activities.

185. Marsh, F. N., & Katz, J. (eds.). (1985). **Biology, Crime and Ethics: A Study of Biological Explanations for Criminal Behavior.** Cincinnati, OH: Anderson Publishing Company, 397 p.

This book discusses: (1) leading theories that support biological perspectives on crime causation, (2) their major criticisms, as well as (3) the ethical, legal, and political ramifications of attempting to control crime based on such theories. The three main parts of the book are: (1) sociobiology, (2) biomedical explanations for crime, and (3) ethical, legal and political considerations arising from biological notions of crime causation. Other issues discussed include: psychosurgery, reproductive controls, biological therapies, and physical interventions to alter behavior in a punitive environment.

186. Mathiesen, T. (1990). **Prison on Trial: A Critical Assessment.** Newbury Park, CA: Sage, 192 p.

This volume examines prisons in the United States and Western Europe throughout the 1980's, with an eye toward the decarceration movement. The author critically evaluates the various arguments which have been advanced in support of imprisonment, including rehabilitation, deterrence, incapacitation, and justice.

187. Miller, M. (1987). *Legal and Ethical Limits on the Use of Predictions of Dangerousness in the Criminal Law.* In Dutile, F. N. and Foust, C. H. (eds.), **Prediction of Criminal Violence.** Springfield, IL: Charles C. Thomas, 35-53.

This chapter identifies the practical uses of dangerousness predictions, examines challenges to the use of statistical predictions in criminal justice, and suggests three principles for the routine use of predictions of dangerousness in the criminal justice system. Customary applications of predictions of dangerousness are widespread and well-accepted in the criminal justice system. They are used in judicial sentencing, police arrest decisions, and prosecutorial decisions about case dispositions. Exceptional uses include preventive and pretrial detention, career criminal investigations, and selective incapacitation. Critics of statistical prediction models of dangerousness argue that such techniques are not sufficiently accurate to form the basis for depriving persons of their liberty, and that they violate the presumption of innocence ideal which forms the heart of the American system of justice.   However, the author recognizes that the use of dangerousness predictions is inevitable in the criminal justice system, and should be made as accurate as possible and limited in application. Twenty-eight notes are provided.

188. Miller, W. P. (1987). *Hunger-Striking Prisoners.* **Journal of Prison and Jail Health,** 6 (1), 40-61.

The author examines what effect international policies have had on the resolution of ethical and moral dilemmas which arise from having to deal with inmates choosing to participate in hunger strikes. United States prison system policies which have a bearing on the issue of hunger strikes are explored. A national consensus of force-feeding these inmates is said to be slowly emerging. The rights of individual hunger strikers are seen as continually challenged by the administration's interests in maintaining its own rights. Administrative interests are said to include: (1) providing for the health and welfare of inmates, and (2) supporting an orderly prison system. The author concludes that experiences in the Western world run counter to the force-feeding of hunger strikers, as mandated by the World Medical Association Declaration of Tokyo.

189. Murphy, J. W. (1990). **Are Prisons Any Better: Twenty Years of Correctional Reform.** Newbury Park, CA: Sage. 184 p.

This collection of readings covers the last two decades of American prison development in the light of various standards which have been advanced to improve the correctional system. Themes useful in improving the system are identified, and crime prevention and correctional reform are stressed.

190. Musheno, M. C., et al. (1987). *Organizational Diffusion of a Correctional Reform.* **Criminal Justice Policy Review,** 2 (2), 174-190.

A Western state's effort to implement a reform policy to professionalize its correctional system is studied. Specifically, a new in-service training program was developed to instill workable professional ethics and practices in the correctional work force. Mixed methods and triangulated data sources were used to study differences in institutional organizational capacity and rates of ethical commitment. This research is part of a larger movement that challenges routine administration and goal fidelity as appropriate constructs for studying social policy reforms. Three tables, six notes, and a 38-item bibliography are included.

191. National Council on Crime and Delinquency. (1984). **Research and Criminal Justice Policy.** San Francisco, CA: National Council on Crime and Delinquency Publications, 161 p.

A series of essays address some of the common ethical falsities in criminal justice research. Topics covered include: (1) ethical dilemmas in predictive sentencing, (2) types of offenders, (3) the moral value of offenders' states of mind, (4) the worth of treatment, and (4) the revitalization of clinical sociology and juvenile diversion programs.

192. Unk. (1984). *Work as an Avenue of Prison Reform.* **New England Journal on Criminal and Civil Confinement,** 10 (1), 45-64.

The right of an inmate to have work, and the right of the system to provide work are underlying issues in corrections according to the author. Putting inmates to work is seen as the basis for a sound rehabilitative program in at least twenty states. Through hard work, inmates are able to pay restitution, learn a trade other than crime, and develop a work ethic. Government is able to reduce its tax on society for the cost of maintaining the correctional system, and businesses are able to gain a reasonable profit from the use of inmate laborers. While work reforms may not flourish in all settings and with all inmates, the majority, it is claimed, will do nothing but good for all parties involved.

193. Ring, C. R. (1987). **Contracting for the Operation of Private Prisons: Pros and Cons.** Laurel, MD: American Correctional Association, 50 p.

An abridged version of the "Prisons for Profit" project, which was prepared by the Massachusetts Legislative Research Bureau, is reviewed. This project was ordered by the General Court of Massachusetts. It analyzed the ethical, financial, legal, and other public policy concerns raised by private prison proposals. The introduction of the profit motive into the prison system is seen as likely to have a serious lessening effect on the accountability, and welfare of inmates. The need for test facilities and for the proper analysis of these test sites is discussed. One table and chapter footnotes are included.

194. Rosenberg, H., et al. (1986). *DUI (Driving Under the Influence) Offenders and Mental Health Service Providers: A Shotgun Marriage?* In Valle, Stephen K. (ed.), **Drunk Driving in America.** New York, NY: Haworth Press, 163-168.

The social, legal and ethical ramifications of dealing with the Driving Under the Influence (DUI) offender in the mental health arena are discussed. The author asserts that rehabilitative systems presently being used, as well as those under development, are inadequate to handle this re-occurring problem. The author maintains that uniformly reliable DUI diagnostic and treatment procedures have not yet been established, and that there remains no assurance that an offender opting for treatment under a mental health program will receive their just desserts.

195. Saunders, D. G. (1988). *Issues in Conducting Treatment Research With Men Who Batter.* In Hotaling, Gerald T., et al. (eds.), **Coping With Family Violence: Research and Policy Perspectives.** Newbury Park, CA: Sage, 145-157.

See Chapter 5, Victim's Rights.

196. Scheurell, R. (1983). *Social Work Ethics in Probation and Parole.* In Roberts, A. R. (ed.), **Social Work in Juvenile and Criminal Justice Settings.** Springfield, IL: Charles C. Thomas, 241-251.

This chapter deals with some of the conflicts that may arise when social work ethics are applied to probation and parole functions within a correctional setting. Of central concern are the individual and multiple level relationships that exist between clients, colleagues, employers, communities, and the social work profession. The author maintains that the important values of client self-determination, confidentiality, and acceptance can be violated by any number of individuals within the correctional setting. A problem at any level can have bad ramifications for the relationship between workers and their clients.

197. Sheldon, J. (1987). *Legal and Ethical Issues in the Behavioral Treatment of Juvenile and Adult Offenders.* In Morris, Edward K., et al. (eds.), **Behavioral Approaches to Crime and Delinquency: A Handbook of Application, Research, and Concepts.** New York, NY: Plenum, 543-575.

This chapter discusses the often unconsidered ethical and legal issues that must be dealt with in the behavioral treatment of juvenile and adult offenders. The legal issues of confidentiality and privacy are discussed. The roles of those involved in treatment programs, the modification of offender behavior, external review of treatment goals, and the professional training of therapists are all discussed. The author maintains that legally safe and ethically humane intervention programs may greatly aid in creating an environment where successful treatments can take place.

198. Smith, F. V. (1984). *Alabama Prison Option: Supervised Intensive Restitution Program.* **Federal Probation,** 48 (1), 32-35.

An introduction to Alabama's Supervised Intensive Restitution (SIR) program is presented. It is a nonresidential treatment program that combines punitive restrictions on freedom with restitutional requirements and the work ethic. Selected inmates are supervised throughout three gradient degrees of supervision by SIR officers. Two SIR officers typically supervise fifty cases. The program is described as having over 800 inmates, and a 5 percent success, and a 19 percent failure rate.

199. Texas Adult Probation Commission. (1983). **Standards for Adult Probation Services in Texas.** Austin, TX: Texas Adult Probation Commission Publications, 41 p.

The Texas Adult Probation Commission adopted this manual of standards for its Adult Probation Services Division. The manual includes a code of ethics for Texas adult probation officers, and provides specific standards in the areas of: administration, probation officer responsibilities, supervision, caseloads, programs, facilities, equipment, fiscal responsibilities, waivers, goals and objectives, intensively supervised probation, and restitution centers, as well as rules for funds distribution.

200. Tonry, M. (1987). *Prediction and Classification: Legal and Ethical Issues.* In Don M. Gottfredson and Michael Tonry (eds.), **Prediction and Classification: Criminal Justice Decision Making.** Chicago, IL: University of Chicago Press, 367-413.

This essay explores the legal and ethical implications of recent moves toward the increased use of: (1) preventive detention, (2) selective incapacitation, and (3) predictions of dangerousness. The author shows that the law and the U.S. Constitution impose few restraints on the criminal justice system's use of prediction and classification. A summary is provided of the debate between those who believe in the limited use of state powers and those who believe the opposite. The author advocates replacing existing criminal codes with new ones that define offenses in greater detail and allow shorter maximum sentences. Tables and approximately 40 references are provided.

201. United Nations. (1984). **Report of the Interregional Preparatory Meeting for the Seventh United Nations Congress on the Prevention of Crime and the Treatment of Offenders on Topic V:**

'Formulation and Application of United Nations Standards and Norms in Criminal Justice.' New York, NY: United Nations Publications, 30 p.

During the Interregional Preparatory Meeting for the Seventh United Nations Congress on the Prevention of Crime and the Treatment of Offenders, discussions centered on the implementation of criminal justice standards and the possible addition of new standards and norms. Steps were taken to assist in a quick and effective implementation of developing standards. Possible additions were identified to include: (1) alternatives to prison, (2) the social resettlement of offenders, (3) independence of the legal profession, (4) the proper role of prosecution, (5) prisoner's rights, and (6) the transfer of criminal proceedings. Alternatives to capital punishment are also discussed.

202. ____. (1986). *Capital Punishment.* **Crime Prevention and Criminal Justice Newsletter,** No. 12-13, special issue (November). Vienna, Austria: United Nations Crime Prevention and Criminal Justice Branch, 67 p.

Twelve papers examine the history and practice of capital punishment, as well as legal and ethical issues related to its imposition and abolition. United Nations action in the field of capital punishment is reviewed, and the efforts of the Council of Europe to promote the abolition of capital punishment are outlined. Historical and contemporary rationales advanced for and against the death penalty are discussed, including deterrence and brutalization arguments. Public opinion toward the death penalty and its status worldwide are also considered. The use of capital punishment in common criminal law, in military law, and as an instrument of national defense is discussed. Major trends in capital punishment research are reviewed in the topical areas of: (1) general debates, (2) legal issues, (3) application, (4) public attitudes, (5) deterrence effectiveness, and (6) the conditions under which death row inmates are held. Additional papers examine capital punishment policies and practices, as well as related issues, in the United States, China, Uruguay, Latin America, Australia, Poland, and Botswana. A list of United Nations documents and resolutions on crime prevention and criminal justice is appended.

203. Urofsky, M.I. (1984). *Right to Die: Termination of Appeal for*

Condemned Prisoners.   **Journal of Criminal Law and Criminology,** 75 (3), 553-582.

According to the author, death-row inmates should have the right to knowingly terminate their appeals process and expedite the completion of their sentence. Courts have generally upheld cases where the inmate knowingly and voluntarily chooses to waive further appeals. This issue runs parallel to the right to die issue when individuals are terminally ill. For various reasons, some inmates choose to waive their right to further appeals and to expedite the completion of their sentence.

204. Vandiver, M., & Radelet, M. L. (1984). **Capital Punishment Project: Bibliography.** Gainsville, FL: University of Florida Sociology Department, 32 p.

This bibliography contains over 450 citations compiled by the Capital Punishment Project at the University of Florida. Citations are presented in four general subject divisions. The section on general and historical information is divided into worldwide, England, America, and Florida subsections. Other sections cover issues of racism, deterrence, clemency, death row confinement, public opinion, effects and methods of execution, and legal issues. Case citations of interest to general readers are provided. The final section provides a bibliography of publications which argue for and against capital punishment on moral and religious grounds. Citations were published between 1889 and 1984.

205. Veneziano, C. A. (1986). *Prison Inmates and Consent to Treatment: Problems and Issues.* **Law and Psychology Review,** (10), 129-146.

Ethical and practical points of view are outlined in case law regarding the rights of inmates to have or refuse treatment. The author suggests that the goal of any correctional system, whether it be primarily rehabilitative or punitive in orientation, encompasses both a right to treatment and a right to refuse treatment. Case law is cited which tends to support inmate autonomy, and which upholds procedures for obtaining informed consent in situations where treatment may be considered serious and intrusive.

206. Verdun-Jones, S. N. (1988). *Right To Refuse Treatment: The Other Side of the Coin.* In Freeman, Richard J., et al. (eds.), **The Treatment of Sexual Aggression: Legal and Ethical Issues.** Burna-

by, BC: Simon Fraser University Criminology Research Centre, 91-124.

> The professional ethics of Canadian mental health physicians are tested by their ability to impose treatments upon involuntarily (civilly) committed mental health patients without consent. Various remedies are presented to prevent physicians from abusing their authority over committed patients.

207. Von Hirsch, A. (1984). *Ethics of Selective Incapacitation: Observations on the Contemporary Debate.* **Crime and Delinquency**, 30 (2), 175-194.

> This article contends that the strategy of selective incapacitation cannot be based upon prediction studies, particularly those relying upon the offender's prior criminal history. According to the author, the criteria for prediction and for desert differ significantly in the degree of emphasis that may be placed on prior criminal history, and in the type of information about that history which may appropriately be used. The article also criticizes recent arguments that desert furnishes only broad outer limits on punishments, within which predictive determinations may fairly be used. It is concluded that the tension between selective incapacitation and desert cannot be ignored, and that the use of selective incapacitation strategies in sentencing entails sacrifices of equity for offenders.

208. _____. (1985). **Past or Future Crimes: Deservedness and Dangerousness in the Sentencing of Criminals.** New Brunswick, NJ: Rutgers University Press, 230 p. NOTE: Crime, Law, and Deviance series.

> In examining the conflict between the just desserts and selective incapacitation theories of sentencing, this book argues that an ethical sentence must be proportional and just, requiring that any incapacitation strategy in sentencing should focus on crime categories rather than particular offenders. An analysis of the just desserts theory explains why and how punishments should be proportionate to the severity of crimes already committed. Also considered are the gauging of crime seriousness, the weighting of current and previous convictions, and the fixing of starting points when constructing a penalty scale. A critique of selective incapacitation reviews recent research on career criminals and demonstrates limitations in predicting serious criminality.

Moral objections to sentencing offenders primarily for their expected future crimes are noted. The book concludes that the only way to meet the standard of proportionality and justice is to sentence offenders by crime categories rather than by predictions of future criminality. A subject index and a 200-item bibliography are provided.

209. Von Hirsch, A., & Gottfredson, D. M. (1984). *Selective Incapacitation: Some Questions About Research Design and Equity.* **New York University Review of Law and Social Change,** 12 (1), 11-51.

In examining two studies of criminality prediction, this paper considers the accuracy of new prediction devices, the validity of claims that predictive sentencing can reduce crime, the ethics of selective incapacitation, and resource allocation issues raised by selective incapacitation. Past successes and failures in forecasting criminality are reviewed, and errors which arose in those studies are highlighted. Included are 139 references.

210. Wilkins, L. T. (1985). *Politics of Prediction.* In David P. Farrington and Roger Tarling (eds.), **Prediction in Criminology.** Albany, NY: State University of New York Press, 34-51.

This paper discusses ethical and policy issues in the development of prediction methods as well as the potential uses of such methods in criminal justice. The moral questions that arise in this area are said to derive from concepts of freedom and democracy, and from efforts to balance individual and state rights. The author holds that moral issues surrounding the use of predictive techniques for persons not yet found guilty (and therefore presumed innocent) are different from those raised by the prediction of recidivism; and that the prediction of recidivism differs morally from the prediction of probable delinquency. The concepts of due process and just deserts are cited as necessary and as providing useful constraints on the over-employment of predictive instruments. Five references are provided.

211. Williams, P. C., et al. (1981). *Ethical Problems: Cases and Commentaries: Health vs. Safety Receiving Needed Care.* **Journal of Prison Health,** 1 (1), 44-55.

A problem case involving the health care of an inmate, his religious rights, and the security of a prison is presented. In the case, the inmate has glaucoma and has to leave the prison in order to receive adequate medical treatment. The prison requires that all inmates entering the prison must be strip-searched. The inmate maintains that it is against his religious beliefs to be subjected to such a search. Two commentaries emphasizing the ethical ramifications of various solutions are also presented.

212. Williamson, H. E. (1990). **The Corrections Profession.** Newbury Park, CA: Sage, 200 p.

This book is intended to provide a one-stop source on information about corrections as a profession. The author notes the lack of a comprehensive work on the corrections profession -- a lack said to be especially significant given the evolution of professionalism in the field over the past few decades. The book seeks to clarify the various professional roles of correctional workers, to articulate the obligations of correctional staffers, and to establish a basis for realistic behavioral choices within the correctional environment.

213. Wish, E. D. (1986). **Identification of Drug Abusing Offenders: A Guide for Practitioners,** Draft Report. Rockville, MD: National Institute of Justice, 25 p.

See Chapter 2, The Police.

5
Victim's Rights

214. Becker, J. V., et al. (1988). *Incest.* In Van Hasselt, Vincent B., et al. (eds.), **Handbook of Family Violence.** New York, NY: Plenum Press, 187-205.

Various aspects relating to the crime of incest are discussed. Among them are: epidemiological findings; origins of the incest taboo; characteristics of the perpetrator, the mother, and victim; treatment issues; case management; a treatment model for the perpetrator; various family issues; legal and ethical issues; and future research directions. Basic and advanced research programs are suggested for obtaining a clearer picture of the true magnitude of this crime and the effectiveness of treatment programs. 66 references are provided.

215. Berlin, F. S., et al. (1986). *Pedophilia: Diagnostic Concepts, Treatment, and Ethical Considerations.* In Haden, Dawn C. (ed.), **Out of Harm's Way: Readings on Child Sexual Abuse, Its Prevention and Treatment.** Phoenix, AZ: Oryx Press, 155-171.

According to the author, examining pedophilia in terms of its etiology, manifestations, diagnosis, and treatment reveals serious clinical and ethical issues. The ability of a pedophile to seek professional help without the fear of being betrayed or shunned is identified as important to successful treatment. The four major types of treatment (psychotherapy, behavior therapy, surgery, and medication) are described. The author suggests that through proper diagnosis, professionalism and treatment the pedophile, as well as society as a whole, will best be served.

216. Bradley, E. J., et al. (1987). *Methodological and Ethical Issues in Child Abuse Research.* **Journal of Family Violence**, 2 (3), 239-255.

A research-oriented review of fundamental ethical and procedural issues in recent child abuse studies is presented in this paper. These issues include: a definition of the population, specific problems under study, sex biases, the recruitment of study subjects, informed consent, deception, and confidentiality. Two major problems are identified as associated with studies of child abuse: first, literature has generally failed to include information that is necessary to accurately assess the procedures and practices used in studies of child abuse; and secondly, in those studies that did include assessment information, the subjects best interests were often overlooked. A table and thirty-three references are provided.

217. Conte, J. R. (1988). *Research on the Prevention of Sexual Abuse of Children.* In Hotaling, Gerald T., et al. (eds.), **Coping With Family Violence: Research and Policy Perspectives**. Newbury Park, CA: Sage Publications, 300-309.

This chapter provides a discussion about methodological and ethical problems that exist in many of the programs that deal with the sexual victimization of children. Concepts commonly considered to be relevant include: (1) acceptable/unacceptable touching, (2) control over access to one's body, and (3) assertive means for responding to abuse. Research programs are described which explore the diverse variables that bear on these projects and the children involved in them. Eleven references are included.

218. Fortune, M. M. (1983). **Sexual Violence: The Unmentionable Sin.** New York, NY: Pilgrim Press, 248 p.

Using traditional ethical sources based upon Christian tradition, the author defines categories of ethical perspectives applicable to the study of sexual violence. Along with the redefining of the various ethical perspectives, a new framework for understanding and responding to sexual violence is presented. A special section is presented for the understanding of the pedophile and the juvenile victim. Guidance is given for pastoral counseling, and strategies for action are presented.

219. Geffner, R., et al. (1988). *Research Issues Concerning Family Violence.* In Van Hasselt, Vincent B., **Handbook of Family Violence.** New York, NY: Plenum Press, 457-481.

The major issues surrounding family violence research are identified as centering around conceptual and methodological designs, as well as treatment evaluations, ethics and future directions. Research methodologies relevant to the study of family violence are discussed, in terms of: sampling, epidemiology, measurement techniques, experimental design and data analysis. The authors discuss ethical concerns related to issues of confidentiality and consent. Areas for future study are identified to include: child physical abuse, child sexual abuse, the appropriate response to child witnesses of family violence, and marital violence including rape. Ninety-three references are provided.

220. Gragg, R. (1986). *Legal and Ethical Considerations.* In Everstine, Diane S., et al. (eds.), **Sexual Trauma in Children and Adolescents: Dynamics and Treatment.** New York, NY: Brunner, Mazel, 174-196.

Ethical and legal issues surrounding the assessment and treatment of sexually abused victims are discussed. The author suggests that children are especially vulnerable victims because they lack sexual knowledge. Ethical issues in dealing with sexual trauma among children are said to include: suspect identification, clinician record-keeping, court procedures, and the prosecutor's decision-making process as it bears on the filing of criminal actions. New laws that clearly define sexual offenses and provide harsh punishments for offenders are advocated.

221. Gross, D. R., et al. (1987). *Ethics, Violence, and Counseling: Hear No Evil, See No Evil, Speak No Evil?* **Journal of Counseling and Development,** 65 (7), 340-344.

According to the author, the counselor's role in dealing with violent clients is surrounded by a variety of ethical and legal issues. Issues identified in this article include: client welfare, dangerousness, confidentiality, the duty to warn others of dangerous clients, and the sexual abuse of clients by counselors. Counselors are advised that professional knowledge and general social awareness are highly necessary skills. Nineteen references are presented.

222. Hall, M. H. (1972). **Non-Accidental Injuries In Children**. London, England: Royal Society of Health, 6 p.

Cases of acute and prolonged child abuse are reviewed. The multipurpose role of the physician is defined as it relates to diagnosis, confidentiality, and criminal justice system involvement. Various verbal and physiomedical sources of evidence available to physicians and other individuals close to victims are discussed. Physician ethics are said to be caught in the nexus between law, social opinion, parental pressure, the child's desires, and personal beliefs.

223. Margolin, G., et al. (1988). *Wife Battering*. In Van Hasselt, Vincent B., **Handbook of Family Violence**. New York, NY: Plenum Press, 89-117.

The frequency, causes, current treatment modalities, ethical, legal, and future issues of relevance to spouse abuse are presented in this paper. Statistics on wife battering are presented. Causes are subsumed under a wide variety of theories. Ethical concerns are identified as centering on the therapist's role in counseling and his or her ability to effectively convince spouses to leave damaging relationships. Fifteen references are provided.

224. Mouzakitis, C. M., & Varghese, R. (eds.). (1985). **Social Work Treatment with Abused and Neglected Children**. Springfield, IL: Charles C. Thomas, 396 p.

An overview of the treatment of abused and neglected children within the social work profession is presented. Special attention is given to the etiological, medical, legal, ethical, and programmatic issues related to child abuse in the United States. Numerous factors that are believed to contribute to child abuse and neglect are discussed. State laws and standards relevant to the handling of abused and neglected children are compared. Extensive references are provided.

225. Pagelow, M. D. (1988). *Marital Rape*. In Van Hasselt, Vincent B., **Handbook of Family Violence**. New York, NY: Plenum Press, 207-232.

The crime of marital rape is defined and the known extent of the crime is reported. State laws of relevance are described, and the future of such laws is debated. Factors which promote the offense are identified as having historic, economic, legal and social dimensions. Service oriented professionals are exhorted to become sensitized to this crime, its victims, offenders, and the ethical issues involved. A great need is said to exist for accurate research in this area. Seventy-eight references are provided.

226. *Prediction of Interpersonal Criminal Violence.* (1988). **Violence and Victims,** 3 (4), 243-330. NOTE: Special issue.

This special issue argues that accurate predictions of interpersonal criminal violence can be made, that public policies can be based on those predictions, and that predictive decision-making is both ethical and legally justifiable. Individual articles in the issue focus on diverse aspects of predicting criminal violence. Dangerousness prediction is discussed in terms of its impact on civil rights, and the pervasive need for both societal protection and predictability in everyday human interaction.

227. Rosenbaum, A. (1986). *Family Violence.* In Curran, William J., et al. (eds.), **Forensic Psychiatry and Psychology.** Philadelphia: F.A. Davis Company, 227-246.

The nature and extent of family violence within the United States is discussed, and the legal and ethical issues it poses for mental health professionals are identified. Relevant states laws, including those designed to protect and remove children as well as spouses from violent households, are described. Each case is said to represent unique ethical dimensions, involving decisions which must be made as to what is truly best for the individual family, the state, and society as a whole. Eighty-four references are provided.

228. Saunders, D. G. (1988). *Issues in Conducting Treatment Research With Men Who Batter.* In Hotaling, Gerald T., et al. (eds.), **Coping With Family Violence: Research and Policy Perspectives.** Newbury Park, CA: Sage Publications, 145-157.

The author maintains that various ethical and practical problems prevent the use of ideal research designs when studying treatment outcomes for programs involving women who are battered by men. Some of the problems include: (1) identifying appropriate treatments for violent and dangerous behavior, (2) the uncontrollable assignment of offenders from court systems to treatment programs, and (3) ethical issues involved in gaining consent for treatment from male offenders. When designing and conducting research on programs in this potentially violent and secretive field, the author suggests that ethical issues should be given primary consideration. Forty-five references are given.

229. Seagull, E. A. (1987). *Child Psychologist's Role in Family Assessment.* In Helfer, Ray E., et al. (eds.), **The Battered Child.** Chicago, IL: University of Chicago Press, 152-173.

The child psychologist's role in family assessment is described in terms of a diversity of issues. The issues include: (1) definitional considerations involving the term "child psychologist," (2) ethical issues in family assessment, (3) characteristics of a successful child protection team, (4) the proper conduct of childhood psychological assessments, and (5) the theraputic role of family interaction. The effective use of psychodiagnostic tests are also discussed. Other ethical issues, such as gaining the patient's informed consent, and his or her right to confidentiality are included. Ninety references are listed.

230. Sheleff, L. S. (1978). **The Bystander: Behavior, Law, Ethics.** Lexington, MA: Lexington Books, 234 p.

This study examines the legal and ethical ramifications of bystander attitudes and actions (or lack thereof) in response to strangers in distress. The work cites research studies, actual cases, and fictitious situations to generate conclusions about the legal and ethical considerations that bystanders must face. Amplified rebound and bonding effects among bystanders are addressed.

231. Walker, L. E. (1986). *Ethical Issues in Family Violence Research.* In Tonry, Michael, et al. (eds.), **Family Violence: A Thematic Issue of Crime and Justice.** Washington, D.C.: National Institute of Justice, 40 p. NOTE: Papers presented at the Working Conference on Family Violence as a Criminal Justice Issue.

According to the author, research in the field of family violence has historically been riddled with inconsistencies, myths and secrets to the extent that a code of ethics should govern all who work in this area. Ethical biases prevalent in the field are identified as arising from gender biases, patriarchal culture, and general misinformation regarding the social sciences. Ethical guidelines are presented to direct researchers in the conduct of accurate and unbiased research.

6

Information Sources for Research on Criminal Justice Ethics

This chapter provides a brief list of data collections, criminal justice abstracting services, libraries, and on-line services of particular interest to researchers and teachers working in the area of criminal justice. Organizations are grouped according to the following categories: (1) indexing and abstracting services, (2) university-related research programs, (3) professional organizations, (4) data repositories and resource centers, and (5) general research organizations. Within these categories, organizations are listed alphabetically, with information provided on contact persons, telephone numbers, addresses, and types of services provided. Those interested in general guidance on library research in criminal justice should refer to: **Criminal Justice Research in Libraries: Strategies and Resources,** by Marilyn Lutzker and Eleanor Ferrall (Westport, CT: Greenwood Press, 1986), or **Finding Criminal Justice in the Library: A Student Manual of Information Retrieval and Utilization Skills,** by Dennis C. Tucker and Frank Schmalleger (Bristol, IN: Wyndham Hall Press, 1991). A more general listing of criminal justice information sources can be had in: Paula R. Goldberg, **A Network of Knowledge: Directory of Criminal Justice Information Sources,** 7ed (Washington, D.C.: National Institute of Justice, 1988), from which many of the sources which follow were first identified.

I. Indexing and Abstracting Services These publications are available in many libraries.

Criminal Justice Abstracts

Abstracting service for criminal justice related periodicals, books, and research reports.

PUBLISHED BY: Willow Tree Press, Inc.
P. O. Box 249
Monsey, NY 10952
TELEPHONE: 914-354-9139

Criminal Justice Periodical Index

Indexes, by author and subject, pertinent criminal justice articles from over 100 periodicals.

PUBLISHED BY: University Microfilms International
300 N. Zeeb Road
Ann Arbor, MI 48106
TELEPHONE: 800-521-0600

Criminology & Penology Abstracts

Abstracts of articles and books, including those from over 30 different countries. Subjects covered are criminological theory and penology. Complements coverage in **Police Science Abstracts**.

PUBLISHED BY: Kugler Publications
P.O. Box 516
Amstelveen
The Netherlands

Police Science Abstracts

International coverage of police and forensic science literature is provided by English language abstracts. Complements coverage in **Criminology and Penology Abstracts**.

PUBLISHED BY: Kugler Publications
P.O. Box 516
Amstelveen
The Netherlands

PAIS Bulletin: Public Affairs Information Service

Indexes English language books, periodicals, government documents, and reports covering a wide variety of public policy issues.

PUBLISHED BY: Public Affairs Information Service
                521 West 43rd Street
                New York, NY 10036
TELEPHONE: 212-736-4161

II. University-Related Research Programs

ORGANIZATION: National Institute for Sentencing Alternatives
ADDRESS: Ford Hall, Second Floor
               Brandeis University
               Waltham, MA 02254
TELEPHONE: 617-736-3980
WRITE OR CALL: Mark D. Corrigan
SERVICES: Services include documents on alternative sentencing
and access to professionals in the field through NISA's network.
PUBLICATIONS: **Restitution and Community Services: An
Annotated Bibliography.**

ORGANIZATION: National Judicial College
ADDRESS: Judicial College Building
               University of Nevada/Reno
               Reno, NV 89557
TELEPHONE: 702-784-6747
WRITE OR CALL: V. Robert Payant, Judge, Associate Dean
SERVICES: NJC offers assistance to state and local courts on the
training of trial judges, and in developing court systems and
management plans to avoid delay and improve data management.
PUBLICATIONS: **Criminal Law Outline** (annual), **Judicial Discretion, Courts and the News Media, Ethics for Judges, Sentencing, Inherent Powers of the Courts**, and **Appellate Opinion Preparation**. Approximately 50,000 books, reports, and documents are
held in the college's collection.

ORGANIZATION: School of Criminology
ADDRESS: Florida State University
               Tallahassee, FL 32306
TELEPHONE: 904-644-4050
WRITE OR CALL: Eugene H. Czajkoski
SERVICES: Services include pure and applied research by faculty
members, evaluation of criminal justice programs, policy and data
analysis, and implementing consultation
PUBLICATIONS: **Journal of Drug Issues.**

ORGANIZATION: Institute of Criminal Law and Procedure
                    Georgetown University
ADDRESS: 605 G St. NW
                    Washington, DC 20001
TELEPHONE: 202-662-9586
WRITE OR CALL: William McDonald
SERVICES: Consultation, data bases on plea bargaining, pretrial
release, victim assistance, and repeat offender laws
PUBLICATIONS: **Plea Bargaining, Police Prosecutor Relations
in the U.S.,** and **Defense Counsel.**

ORGANIZATION: Harvard Law School
ADDRESS: Center for Criminal Justice
                    Cambridge, MA 02138
TELEPHONE: 617-495-4457
WRITE OR CALL: Daniel McGillis
SERVICES: Researchers at the Center for Criminal Justice publish books and articles on their work. The Center occasionally
distributes mimeographed working papers dealing with research
findings. The Center's annual report is distributed every December, and summarizes the publications of Center personnel during
the preceding fiscal year.
PUBLICATIONS: Access to Harvard Law School Library. Publication list available.

ORGANIZATION: Department of Criminology
                    Center for Research in Criminology
                    Indiana University of Pennsylvania
                    Indiana, PA 15705-1075
TELEPHONE: 412-357-2720
WRITE OR CALL: Dr. Chris Zimmerman, Randy Martin
SERVICES: Active participation in research related to criminology and criminal justice. The CRC provides consultants for national, state and local criminal justice agencies. Technical support is
provided upon request. The CRC also acts as an information
dissemination center.
PUBLICATIONS: **The Criminal Justice Policy Review.**

ORGANIZATION: Center for Study of Crime, Delinquency
                    and Corrections
ADDRESS: Southern Illinois University at Carbondale
                    Carbondale, Ill 62901
TELEPHONE: 618-453-5701
WRITE OR CALL: Joseph S. Coughlin, Professor
SERVICES: The Center for the Study of Crime, Delinquency, and
Corrections, in addition to its undergraduate and graduate degree

programs conducts research, provides consultation, and develops and implements training programs through contractual arrangements.
PUBLICATIONS: Publications list available.

ORGANIZATION: The Institute for Criminal Justice Ethics
ADDRESS: John Jay College
                          444 West 56th Street
                          New York, NY 10019
TELEPHONE: 212-237-8000, ext. 8033.
WRITE OR CALL: Karen Lerner, Yurong Zahng
SERVICES: The Institute for Criminal Justice Ethics organizes conferences, provides bibliographical services through the cooperation of the John Jay College Library, and is developing a training program in police ethics that can be used by law enforcement academies across the nation.
PUBLICATIONS: **Criminal Justice Ethics** (biannually).

III. Professional Organizations

ORGANIZATION: Academy of Criminal Justice Sciences
ADDRESS: 402 Nunn Hall
                          Academy of Criminal Justice Sciences
                          Northern Kentucky University
                          Highland Heights, KY 41076-1448
TELEPHONE: 606-572-5634
CALL OR WRITE: Patricia DeLancey, Executive Secretary
SERVICES: The Academy provides publications on various aspects of criminal justice education through the Joint Commission on Criminology and Criminal Justice Education. It also produces model curricula for courses.
PUBLICATIONS: **ACJS Today** (bimonthly newsletter); **Justice Quarterly** (quarterly journal); **Journal of Criminal Justice Education**; and the **Issues in Crime and Justice Series** (published under the auspices of Anderson Publishing Co.).

ORGANIZATION: American Bar Association
                          Center for Professional Responsibility
ADDRESS: 750 North Lakeshore Drive
                          Chicago, IL 60611
TELEPHONE: 313-988-5296
WRITE OR CALL: Ms. Marnette Smith
SERVICES: Various articles and publications for the legal profession are offered. New model standards in various fields are also

available. Reference services and publications are for sale.
PUBLICATIONS: Publications list available upon request.

ORGANIZATION: American Correctional Association
ADDRESS: 8025 Laurel Lakes Road
                    Laurel, MD 20707
TELEPHONE: 301-206-5100
WRITE OR CALL: Anthony P. Travisono
SERVICES: ACA offers education, training, and technical assist-
ance to promote professional development and improved practices.
Cost of services reflect effort involved.
PUBLICATIONS: **Corrections Today,** and **On the Line** (bimonth-
ly newsletter). Directories: **Juvenile and Adult Correctional
Departments, Institutions, Agencies and Paroling Authorities;
National Jail and Adult Detention Directory; Probation and Parole
Directory; Proceedings of the Annual Congress of Corrections.**

ORGANIZATION: American Society of Criminology
ADDRESS: Suite 212
                    1314 Kinnear Rd.
                    Columbus, Ohio 43212
TELEPHONE: 614-292-9207
WRITE OR CALL: Sarah Hall, Administrator
SERVICES: The Society fosters research, training, and education
within academic and private institutions as well as within divisions
of the criminal justice system.
PUBLICATIONS: **Criminology: an Interdisciplinary Journal**
(quarterly), and **The Criminologist** (bimonthly newsletter).

ORGANIZATION: American Society for Public Administration
                    Section on Criminal Justice Administration
ADDRESS: c/o Secretariat
                    445 West 59th St.
                    New York, NY 10019
TELEPHONE: 212-489-5027/5024
WRITE OR CALL: Lotte Feinberg
SERVICES: SCJA provides a forum for members to discuss as-
pects of criminal justice (law, administration, research, policy).
The newsletter provides interviews, book reviews, discussions of
current issues, and an information exchange for members.
PUBLICATIONS: **The Key** (quarterly newsletter); **Criminal
Justice Review** (journal).

ORGANIZATION: Commission on Accreditation for Law
                    Enforcement Agencies

ADDRESS: 4242-B Chain Bridge Rd.
                    Fairfax, VA 22030
TELEPHONE: 703-352-4225
WRITE OR CALL: Frank J. Leahy, Assistant Director
SERVICES: The Commission responds to telephonic or mail inquires about the standards of public law enforcement agencies. The Commission updates and re-issues the **Standards for Law Enforcement Agencies** from time to time. Requests involving major research may not be accommodated.
PUBLICATIONS: **Standards for Law Enforcement Agencies; Accreditation Program Book**; and **Accreditation Program Overview**.

ORGANIZATION: Crime and Justice Foundation
ADDRESS: 95 Berkeley Street
                    Boston, MA 02116
TELEPHONE: 617-426-9800
WRITE OR CALL: John Larivee, Deputy Director
SERVICES: The Foundation provides direct assistance to develop and operate mediation and other programs, staff assistance on research projects and requests for information, and assistance in the use of criminal justice library publications. The Foundation sponsors seminars and makes presentations on criminal justice issues for professionals, students, and the general public
PUBLICATIONS: **The Constitutional Rights of Prisoners**; others.

ORGANIZATION: International Association of Chiefs of Police
ADDRESS: 1110 N. Glebe Road
                    Arlington, VA 22201
TELEPHONE: 301-243-6500
WRITE OR CALL: Dan Rosenblatt
SERVICES: Provides consultant surveys, law enforcement research, training aids such as textbooks, audiovisual programs, and a network of training programs. The IACP assists police departments in improving their services. Each activity of the Association supports another. Consultant services may serve as data base leads to research projects in the law enforcement field.
PUBLICATIONS: **The Police Chief, Journal of Police Science and Administration**; others.

ORGANIZATION: National Association for Crime
                    Victim's Rights
ADDRESS: P.O. Box 16161
                    Portland, OR 97216
TELEPHONE: 503-252-9012
WRITE OR CALL: R. L. Montee

SERVICES: Limited research projects, telephone referrals, victim counseling.
PUBLICATIONS: Cases and victim's rights materials.

ORGANIZATION: National Association of Criminal
Justice Planners
ADDRESS: 1511 K. St. N.W.
Washington, DC 20005
TELEPHONE: 202-347-0501
WRITE OR CALL: Mark A Cunniff
SERVICES: Assistance and information to criminal justice planners are given through newsletters, meetings and telephone communications.
PUBLICATIONS: Newsletter (bimonthly) Annual Conference proceedings. **Beyond Crime: Law Enforcement Operational and Cost Data.**

ORGANIZATION: National Council of Juvenile and
Family Court Judges
ADDRESS: P.O. Box 8978
University Station
Reno, NV 89507
TELEPHONE: 702-784-6012
WRITE OR CALL: As appropriate for requester's needs
SERVICES: Research and training services are provided.
PUBLICATIONS: **Juvenile and Family Court Journal; Juvenile and Family Law Digest; Juvenile and Family Court Newsletter.** Textbook and monograph series.

ORGANIZATION: National Legal Aid & Defender Association
ADDRESS: Eighth Floor
1625 K. St. NW
Washington, DC 20006
TELEPHONE: 202-452-0620
WRITE OR CALL: Staff
SERVICES: Services include periodic publications list, bibliographical information, telephone referrals, and on-site technical assistance.
PUBLICATIONS: Data base of technical assistance reports; bibliography of criminal defense related publications.

ORGANIZATION: National Organization for Victim Assistance
ADDRESS: 1757 Park Rd. NW
Washington, DC 20010
TELEPHONE: 202-232-6682

WRITE OR CALL: Dr. Marlene Young
SERVICES: NOVA sponsors an annual conference, the National Forum on Victim Rights, and an information clearinghouse.
PUBLICATIONS: Various books, reports, and documents.

ORGANIZATION: Religious Council of America, Inc.
National Prison Reform Advisory Board
ADDRESS: Suite 603
147 West 42nd St.
NY, NY 10036
TELEPHONE: 212-947-0949
WRITE OR CALL: Ernest Norman Steele, Jr., Executive Director
SERVICES: The Board has a library of updated materials on United States correctional systems; listings of all registered attorneys within the United States and some other countries, of legal aid within the nation; of major corporations who hire ex-offenders; governmental listings of employment opportunities for clients; and major hot line information those in distress.
PUBLICATIONS: **The Prison Reform Magazine; Doing Time Magazine; Alternatives to Incarceration; Retribution or Rehabilitation; Sexual Behavior in Prisons; Youth Crime--The Problem and Some Answers; The Bible and Capital Punishment;** and the **Prisoner's Yellow Pages.**

IV. Data Repositories and Resource Centers

ORGANIZATION: National Archive of Criminal Justice Data
ADDRESS: c/o Inter-university Consortium for
Political & Social Research
P. O. Box 1248
Ann Arbor, MI 48106
TELEPHONE: 800-999-0960 or 313-763-5011
WRITE OR CALL: Victoria Schneider or Zack W. Allen, Jr.
SERVICES: The Archive is continually functioning to process the most relevant criminal justice data sets for use by the research community. The Archive also maintains a staff capable of assisting in the substantive and technical areas of criminal justice research. Data sets are available without charge to researchers affiliated with the 300 universities that are members of ICPSR. Additionally, the Archive provides a yearly summer seminar to interested users.
PUBLICATIONS: **Criminal Justice Data Directory; Criminal Justice Archive and Information Network Newsletter.**

ORGANIZATION: National Institute of Corrections
Information Center
ADDRESS: Boulder, CO
TELEPHONE: 303-939-8866
WRITE OR CALL: Staff
SERVICES: Information services are provided by the NIC Information Center in Boulder Colorado. The NIC seeks to advance the practice of corrections and aid in the development of a more effective, humane, safe, and just correctional system.
PUBLICATIONS: Access to NIC Information Center.

ORGANIZATION: National Institute of Justice
National Criminal Justice Reference Service
ADDRESS: Box 6000
Rockville, MD 20850
TELEPHONE: 800-732-3277 or 301-251-5500
WRITE OR CALL: Customer Service
SERVICES: The National Criminal Justice Reference Service provides information on thousands of government and private publications of interest to the criminal justice community. The toll free telephone lines are operated by reference specialists knowledgeable in various criminal justice subject areas. The reference service reading room is open to the public. Interlibrary loan, audiovisual loans, microfiche, and data base searches are also offered. The reference service operates an electronic bulletin board for quick and easy access to current news and announcements from the Bureau of Justice Statistics and the Justice Statistics Clearinghouse (call 301-738-8895; modem parameters: 8-N-1). The NIJ/NCJRS/BJS data base is also available on DIALOG. NCJRS maintains current bibliographies in special topical areas, and will conduct individualized computer searches of its vast database for anyone with special interests.
PUBLICATIONS: Enormous collection in various forms. **NIJ Reports** (six times per year) abstracts both private and government criminal justice publications.

ORGANIZATION: Graduate Library for Public Affairs
State Univ. of New York at Albany
ADDRESS: 1400 Washington Ave.
Albany, NY 12222
TELEPHONE: 518-442-3300
WRITE OR CALL: Henry Mendelsohn/Richard Irving/Nadia Si
SERVICES: The Library offers both traditional and non-traditional library services. Reference services include legal reference and computer-based literature searches. It is rapidly becoming a regional resource center for academic criminal justice and social welfare studies. Computer based searches are offered for a fee.

PUBLICATIONS: Books, reports, over 5,000 documents. Micro-form Collection: Crime and delinquency Microfiche and NCJRS Microfiche collection

V. General Research Organizations

ORGANIZATION: John Howard Association
ADDRESS: 67 E. Madison St.
Suite 1416
Chicago, IL 60603
TELEPHONE: 312-263-1901
WRITE OR CALL: Marie DiSomma
SERVICES: State master plans for correctional facilities.
PUBLICATIONS: Surveys and Studies.

ORGANIZATION: Police Executive Research Forum
ADDRESS: 2300 M St. N.W.
Washington, DC 20037
TELEPHONE: 202-466-7820
WRITE OR CALL: Martha R. Plotkin
PUBLICATIONS: **Solving Crimes: The Investigation of Burglary and Robbery; How to Rate Your Local Police; Differential Police Response Strategies; Managing Case Assignments; Burglary Investigation Decision Model Replication; Police Collective Bargaining Agreements; A National Management Survey; Survey of Police Operational and Administrative Practices; Responding to Spouse Abuse and Wife Beating;** others.

ORGANIZATION: National Center on Institutions and
Alternatives
ADDRESS: 635 Slaters Lane
Alexandria, VA 22314
TELEPHONE: 703-684-0373
WRITE OR CALL: Herbert Holter
SERVICES: The Center provides client-specific planning and an individual alternative planning service. Costs are on a sliding scale basis.
PUBLICATIONS: **Institutions, Etc.** (monthly newsletter); bibliographies on juvenile violence and deinstitutionalization; and others.

ORGANIZATION: Search Group Inc.
ADDRESS: Suite 145
7311 Greenhaven Dr.

Sacramento, CA 95831
TELEPHONE: 916-392-2550
WRITE OR CALL: Judy Ryder
SERVICES: SEARCH offers technical assistance as well as train-
ing and education in information systems and policy. SEARCH
has a data base (Automated Index of Criminal Justice Information
Systems).
PUBLICATIONS: Compendium of victim/witness   legislation,
compendium of state privacy and security legislation, and digest of
case law on the handling of criminal record information.
Directory of Criminal Justice Information Systems.

ORGANIZATION: Vera Institute of Justice Inc.
ADDRESS: 377 Broadway
                          New York, NY 10016
TELEPHONE: 212-334-1300
WRITE OR CALL: Susan Rai, Sr. Planner/Dr. Sally Hillsman
SERVICES: Staff members will provide written material, answer
questions, and participate in symposia or other programs related to
the Institute's work.
PUBLICATIONS: Reports of past research and surveys.

Author Index

Numbers following entries, in roman type, refer to entry numbers; italicized numbers refer to pages.

Subject Index

Numbers following entries, in roman type, refer to entry numbers; italicized numbers refer to pages. Entries that are printed in capital letters refer to publications.

About the Compilers

FRANK SCHMALLEGER is Chairman of the Department of Sociology, Social Work and Criminal Justice at Pembroke State University in Pembroke, North Carolina. He is the author of many books including *Criminal Justice Today* and edits the series *Criminal Justice in the Twenty-First Century.* As editor of *Ethics in Criminal Justice, The Social Basis of Criminal Justice,* and as founding editor of the journal *The Justice Professional,* he has worked to focus attention within the justice field on ethical concerns.

ROBERT McKENRICK is a graduate of the Police Administration program at Eastern Kentucky University. He received his graduate degree from Webster University in security management. Formerly a military intelligence officer in the U.S. Army's XVIII Airborne Corps, he is presently attending the Temple University School of Law.